DON GIOVANNI

and

IDOMENEO

UNIVERSE OPERA GUIDES

W. A. MOZART

Don Giovanni

*

Idomeneo

Introduction by Anthony Burgess

UNIVERSE BOOKS
New York

Published in the United States of America in 1971 by
Universe Books, 381 Park Avenue South, New York,
N.Y. 10016

Introduction © Anthony Burgess 1971

Library of Congress Catalog Card Number: 71-162693

ISBN 0-87663-151-0

Devised and produced by Norton Bailey Ltd., 103
Lonsdale Road, London, S.W.13
Printed in Great Britain

CONTENTS

Introduction

People who gain their notions of the character of musical genius from romantic literature, seeing composers as wild-haired piano-smashers, volcanoes of temperament, monomaniacs who go their own way, must cleanse their minds of such images before confronting Wolfgang Amadeus Mozart. The composer as angelic brute is an attractive fictional property, and it made a best-seller of Margaret Kennedy's *The Constant Nymph*. But only in the nineteenth century did composers fulfil the twentieth-century popular novelists' view of the archetypal composer. There were a few men who were, like Byron, bigger than life – Berlioz, with his opium-dreams and his thousand-piece orchestra; Wagner, whose huge Aryan visions were indulged by a mad king; Liszt, the womanizing abbé with his warts and white mane and cigars and magic keyboard. Before them came Beethoven, the true source of the archetype, who was a deaf colossus with terrible manners and an artistic single-mindedness that had never been known before. With him, the creation of music as the emanation of one's own personality, and not as artefacts made primarily for the enjoyment of others, accorded with the new romantic doctrines of Feeling and the revolutionary slogans about Liberty.

In previous centuries it had been very different. The musical composer had usually been a kind of upper servant, tied to a cathedral or an aristocratic court, ordered to write motets or minuets as his patron, bishop or prince, dictated. There was neither room nor time for temperament. Temperament, anyway, has always been primarily an attribute of executants, not creators. Singers especially are traditionally notorious for rages, sulks, and an intransigence before which mere composers must bow, unless they are called Beethoven or Lewis Dodd. Generally, the smaller the vocal talent the bigger the head.

Mozart was very much a child of the eighteenth century, when, as Jean-Jacques Rousseau saw, everybody was in chains and ready for a new deal or social contract. In England, that period was notable for Grub-street writers looking desperately for patrons (Dr. Johnson, who anticipated Beethoven, abandoned vassalage and struck out on his own). In the Habsburg Empire, it was notable for mediocre musicians trying to be salaried Kapellmeisters. That Empire was full of small aristocratic and episcopal courts, and these had to have music as they had to have art galleries and livery stables. A resident choir, organist and orchestra must be available for religious routine and secular junketing. Mass in the morning, a ball at night, a wedding to be solemnized, a triumphant return from the Grand Tour loudly TeDeumed. There were also concerts, with symphonies and virtuoso fireworks on solo instruments, but these were always private affairs, the notion of the public concert being a free-enterprise and democratic one and the times not yet ripe for it. The Habsburg Empire cultivated music diligently, but only as an aspect of the full aristocratic life.

With so many musicians around, one would have expected — fulfilling the statistical law — a flowering of musical genius. But such genius, meaning powerful originality and a strong individual vision, cannot easily come to birth in an environment where the artist's status is low and his function prescribed and circumscribed. It is not easy to imagine Beethoven's Ninth Symphony getting as far even as a first rehearsal in the court of the Archbishop-Elector at Bonn. Let music be kept in its proper station, and symphonies be tuneful and short. Eighteenth-century genius had to be considerable in order to manifest itself through routine jobs and speedy commissions (a week for a concerto, a month for an opera). Mozart's genius was very great indeed, and its greatness is attested by its civilized submission to accepted forms, even clichés. To shrug, smile, and still be a genius is granted to few. Mozart wrote for society, not for himself, but every bar of his mature work is instinct with his own personality. Sometimes, especially in such late works as the final symphonies, his genius threatened to smash the accepted forms in a Beethovenian way. Occasionally this genius made his lordly listeners uneasy; there is always a subversive whiff in a work of genius, its recognition glossed as failure to understand. But, for the most part, Mozart made himself very clearly understood; he had a supreme talent as well as a towering genius, and this talent was in the service of giving pleasure.

Mozart was born into the world of musical servitude. His father,

8

Leopold, was a violinist and small composer in the court of the Archbishop Sigismund von Schrattenbach at Salzburg. He and his wife Maria Anna produced seven children, but only two survived – Wolfgang Amadeus, born in 1756, and Marianne, nicknamed Nannerl, born in 1751. Both children showed considerable talent at an early age, but Wolfgang was, as all the world knows, a prodigy. At the age of three he was picking out thirds on the keyboard, at four he was playing the clavier, at five he was composing. His sheer musicality is attested in various legends – his fainting when first hearing a trumpet, his ability to distinguish between microtones (or minute divisions of the semitone), a faculty for reproducing from memory – at the keyboard or on paper – a complex composition heard once only. He and his sister were, inevitably, exploited by their father, who took them on concert tours to Munich, Vienna, London, Brussels, Paris, They were kissed and cosseted wherever they went, and Leopold Mozart, whose archiepiscopal master was very indulgent, took them everywhere. Youth's a stuff will not endure, and youthful genius does not always turn into mature genius. So Leopold drove both his children hard, but his son especially hard.

At seven Wolfgang was playing the violin; at eleven he wrote part of an oratorio, his first two symphonies, and four piano concertos, which, in the free and easy manner of the time, he made out of the piano sonatas of other composers. At twelve he was commissioned by the Emperor Joseph II himself to write a comic opera – *La finta semplice*. And at the house of the father of mesmerism, Dr. Franz Mesmer, the still delightful operetta *Bastien und Bastienne* was performed. Back in Salzburg, the Archbishop, aware of what talent he had vicariously bred, set Mozart to composing masses and other church compositions. But Leopold's feet itched to be on the road again, and his palm itched too: young geniuses must be seen as much as heard.

Verona, Milan, Bologna, Rome, Naples, Venice – Italy took Wolfgang to its heart, and Wolfgang's German-Austrian blood became tempered by the spirit of musical Italy: Italian became one of his languages and, very important, libretti in Italian were to inspire his greatest vocal-dramatic flowering. He was starting to take the writing of opera seriously now, but works like *Lucio Silla,* presented in Milan, achieved no large success. *La finta giardiniera* did well in Munich, with the Electress and the Dowager Electress crying *Bravo* and the common sort shouting *Viva Maestro,* but it was only a prentice work.

Mozart the opera-maker needed a real librettist. He also needed to grow up and learn about human passion and intrigue.

Growing up presented its own problems. Not only the problem of love (Mozart, like most heterosexual artists, was susceptible to women, and the ladies of the aristocratic courts were inflammatory charmers), but the problem of finding a niche in the adult world. The time is short for being an infant prodigy. There were plenty of boys of nineteen who could touch the clavier divinely, but there were few of nine who could play it even moderately. And a dashed-off opera, like the *Il rè pastore* Mozart had to write for his Archbishop, would be regarded as no large achievement for a young man touching twenty, not to be compared with a lisping child's derivative minuets. The glamour was going; the hard work had to begin. The Archbishop at Salzburg, once flattered by the compliments of Munich and Vienna on having so brilliant a musician in, or rather out of, his court, seemed ill-disposed to the mature young Mozart. So Mozart began to look for openings elsewhere.

He tried for a post in Bologna but had no luck. Conditions at Salzburg deteriorated, and, when Mozart asked the Archbishop for new leave of absence, His Grace suggested that he and his father take permanent leave. At this Leopold Mozart exhibited the fright of an ageing employee. But the capricious cleric later assured him that his services were still required and let Wolfgang, accompanied by his mother, again go off on his travels. The boy wrote home regularly, as he had always done, and revealed in his letters the sense of fun that was to give such a champagne sparkle to his mature operas. He had the eye of the dramatist; he observed. He sums up with something like literary skill the absurdity of Graf, who wrote only flute concertos: 'His words are all on stilts and he generally opens his mouth before he knows what he wants to say; and often it shuts again without having done anything'. He is not only sharp and funny; he is frequently obscene. The whole family had a teutonic obsession with farts and faeces, and Mozart revelled, after putting notes of airy delicacy on paper, in gross lavatory mirth, 'My hole itches,' he says. 'Perhaps some shit wants to come out.' And then back to the creation of more aethereal emanations.

Mozart sought a post at Mannheim, but his father told him that musicians were poorly paid there. Still, said the son, there were clarinets in the orchestra, which they didn't have at Salzburg. There was something more than clarinets; there was the beautiful young singer Aloysia Weber, who sang Mozart's music divinely. Mozart fell in love with her and had no wish to leave Mannheim. His father, scenting that his son was making little money and fooling about instead of paying paternal debts (for this leave of absence had required heavy capitalising), tried to send him to Paris, but the attractions of Mannheim prevailed and begot an uncharacteristic unfiliality. When, at last, mother and son went to seek their father's fortune in Paris, the young composer became acquainted with true grief, not the fictitious emotion of conventional opera. His mother died. Later his pain was compounded by the refusal of Aloysia Weber to take his love seriously: she became a singer at the Munich court opera, well paid, too good for a mere composer. All this was part of Mozart's growing up.

At the age of twenty-three he was back in Salzburg. There was a new Archbishop there — Hieronymus Colloredo — and Mozart settled to a life of musical service in the court. A good deal of music he wrote fails to reflect the spirit of the patronising commission — such free and original works as the Sinfonia Concertante for violin, viola and orchestra, for instance, and the Concerto for two pianos. But he had still produced no great masterpiece. A year after his appointment — in 1780 — the chance to display his genius in an extended work came at last, and it came only indirectly from Salzburg. 1780 is the year of *Idomeneo*.

Opera was essentially an Italian art-form. England developed its own sturdy operatic tradition out of the masque, producing in Purcell's *Dido and Aeneas* (1689) a universal masterpiece, but the rest of the world was very un-English, meaning Italian. Composers like Alessandro Scarlatti, Porpora, Pergolesi and Cimarosa particularized Italian to Neapolitan, and librettists like Zeno and Metastasio laid down the standard verbal requirements. Scarlatti was very ready to taxonomize Neapolitan opera into permanent rigidities, decreeing that opera seria should not merely be serious but marbly monumental, and that opera buffa should be light and funny and racy. Operatic song had to be in the form of the *da capo* aria, meaning a melody stated and, after some bars of contrast, repeated. The dialogue was, of course, sung, but in a stylised form intended to convey the freedom and rapidity of speech — in other words, recitative. The run-of-the-mill recitative was called *secco* (or dry) and had a minimal harpsichord accompaniment; the more dramatic recitative was *stromentato,* or orchestrated. Scarlatti was a considerable composer, and was able to animate the set

11

forms with a strong dramatic thrust and a high lyricism; with lesser composers, it all became a matter of vocal showing-off — icing piped on to bread pudding. Singing prevailed over acting, and the *castrati,* men who had had, as boys, their testicles sacrificed on the altar of art, shrilled out the main male parts in *opera seria,* doing in vocal fireworks what they could not do in bed.

In England, Handel tried to breathe back life into the empty Italian forms, but he failed and turned to oratorio — *opera seria* or even *religiosa* without stage action. In France, Gluck stuck to the stage but rebelled powerfully against pyrotechnics and tyrannical *castrati. Orfeo* appeared in 1762 and introduced, in addition to firm dramatic action and emotion sincerely expressed, two properties which Scarlatti had regarded as unnecessary — the chorus and the ballet. Librettists and composers, especially in England, France and Germany, began to see that opera could be true drama as well as true song, and they developed a medium in which there was scope for convincing spoken dialogue — the ballad opera in England, the *opéra comique* in France, the *Singspiel* in Germany. It was from this speech-song hybrid (examples of which are *The Beggar's Opera* and *Die Zauberflöte*) that the romantic national opera of the nineteenth century was able to proceed. *Opera seria* and *opera buffa* were, in a sense, *castrati:* they filled the eighteenth-century stage but could not breed. Stravinsky's *The Rake's Progress* is, like most of his work, genius happy in pastiche, a deliberate return to the *opera buffa* as Mozart was to practise it in *Don Giovanni.* The rest of twentieth-century opera is derived from Wagner. The *Singspiel* survives as musical comedy.

Idomeneo is *opera seria,* very *seria,* which has taken advantage of the reforms of Gluck. The chorus has important work to do; there is a ballet; there are marches in the French style; there is even a subterranean voice with trombones in the manner of the Oracle in Gluck's *Alceste.* But the music is wholly Mozartian. The commission came from the Elector Carl Theodor, who had known Mozart's work when the electoral court was at Mannheim. Now it had moved to Munich, whose carnival in 1781 was to be marked not only by false noses but by an *opera seria.* Mozart seemed the Elector's best election for composer; as he was stationed in Salzburg, it was considered that he ought to have a Salzburg librettist to work with. And so the Abbé Giambattista Varesco, chaplain to the Archbishop himself, undertook to provide — out of a small but undeniable poetic talent and a rather large ignorance of the requirements of the operatic stage — a suitably weighty text.

The Imperial Poet Metastasio, a pretty enough versifier and a very skilled librettist, was the best model that any tyro could take when planning the book of an opera. What Metastasio taught whole generations of poets was that there was not room for very much poetry in a good libretto: the music was doing the poet's work, the poet must humble himself and regard his texts as a mere handmaid. Metastasio knew the virtues of conciseness and directness, but Varesco, who dutifully read Metastasio, could not believe that words should so abase themselves. After all, religion was based on the Word, not the song, and Varesco was primarily a man of God. He produced a libretto which was far too impracticable for the mechanics of the eighteenth-century stage, and he complained bitterly when Mozart proposed that his lines be drastically cut. Out of this quarrel, out of the need to decide for himself what words could and could not be used, Mozart became his own best man of the theatre. He could make the drama if others would feed him situations and a few, a very few, words.

To give the Abbé his due, the material he chose was far from bad. His *Idomeneo, Re di Creta* was based on a theme essentially biblical and hence well enough known — the story of Jephtha, who returned from the wars and made a vow to sacrifice to Jehovah the first creature he met. This was, as Hamlet reminds us, his own daughter (what a treasure had he, etc.). Varesco turned Jephtha into Idomeneo, King of Crete. He comes home from the Trojan wars, from which he has sent on in advance Ilia, daughter of Priam, as one of his prisoners. Pursued by the wrath of Poseidon, the sea-god, he vows to sacrifice to him the first living being he meets if only he will abate the fury of the storm and let him land safely. And so he reaches shore, encountering not a daughter but a son, Idamante. He does not dare reveal his vow and is, very properly, in extreme anguish. His confidant Arbace recommends that he permit Idamante to escape the danger by escorting Electra, daughter of Agamemnon, to Argos. Electra, improbably, has taken refuge in Crete after the murder of her mother. But Poseidon, being a god, realizes what is afoot and unleashes a new and more terrible storm at the moment of the refugees' departure. He does more: he sends a ghastly sea-monster which, in good classical Sphingine fashion, ravages the kingdom. Idamante goes forth to slay the beast, but the Cretan people, sorely and, as they see it, unfairly tried, come seeking the man who has offended the god and brought all this trouble on themselves.

Idomeneo has to reveal the terrible secret, disclosing the name of his son as the necessary sacrificial victim. The priests make ready for the oblation, but Idamante returns, having killed the monster. Nevertheless, hearing of his father's vow, he is prepared to be slain on the altar. The prisoner Ilia, who loves Idamante, offers to take his place. Poseidon is pleased by this literal self-sacrifice, or intention of it, and the voice of an oracle is heard, stating that Idomeneo had better abdicate and hand over the throne to Idamante and, as his consort, Ilia. There is great rejoicing, except from Electra, who ends as she began, raging, jealous, unwanted. Metastasio might have tied things up neatly by marrying her to Idomeneo, but Varesco liked that sour note in the final concord. It is, in fact, a rather palatable acerbity, like a dash of good vinegar.

The story, then, is good, but Varesco's original script is verbose. He seems to have been unable to imagine the effect on the stage of a musical setting of his words as they stood. Mozart was, as always, very reasonable in his objections, but Varesco proved haughty and difficult. He insisted that he be paid extra for alterations and that, to show he was a victim of a mutilating musician, his script be published, if not performed, exactly as he wrote it. Mozart and he would not communicate with each other directly but used Leopold as an intermediary. As was his usual plan when composing an opera, Mozart wrote the earlier portion and then left a gap before completing the work. It was better to take a mere part of a new opera to rehearsals, and then finish it while the rehearsals proceeded. In that way the composer could see exactly what the performers were capable of doing, and the opera gained from the composer's awareness of the exigencies of cast and orchestra. So, fortunately for us, Mozart was away in Munich during the writing of much of *Idomeneo,* which meant that he had to commit to paper, in letters to his father in Salzburg, his problems and triumphs. We have a revealing record of the making of the opera.

Mozart shows himself a very astute stage-man. He saw that the work could not begin, as it does in Varesco's libretto, with Idomeneo scrambling up rocks at the rear of the stage after his shipwreck. It was absurd of Varesco to write run-on lines and stick asides into arias. In the *da capo* aria there had to be strophic regularity, and the repetition of an aside — imposed by the need to repeat the main melody — could only sound ridiculous. Here, in extenso, is an example of Mozart's good sense:

Tell me, don't you think that the speech of the subterranean voice is too long? Consider it carefully. Picture to yourself the theatre, and remember that the voice must be terrifying — must penetrate — that the audience must believe that it really exists. Well, how can this effect be produced if the speech is too long, for in this case the listeners will become more and more convinced that it means nothing. If the speech of the Ghost in Hamlet were not so long, it would be far more effective. It is quite easy to shorten the speech of the subterranean voice and it will gain thereby more than it will lose.

And again,

After the mourning chorus the king and all his people go away; and in the following scene the directions are 'Idomeneo prostrates himself in the temple'. That is quite impossible. He must come in with his whole suite. A march must be introduced here, and I have therefore composed a very simple one for two violins, viola, cello and two oboes, to be played *a mezza voce*. While it is going on, the king appears and the priests prepare the offerings for the sacrifice. The king then kneels down and begins the prayer.

Not only did Mozart have the pigheadedness of Varesco to deal with; the singers, at least the male ones, gave trouble. The tenor Raeff took the title-part, but he was getting on in years — sixty-five — and very set in his ways. He obstructed, with the best of intentions, all Mozart's attempts to follow new and original paths, and he did not fail to draw on his long, but dated, experience in the theatre in order to give the young composer time-wasting homilies. Moreover, though he was still a fine singer, he could not act. Panzacchi, the other tenor, knew something of acting, but he insisted on his having the part of the confidant Arbace loaded with irrelevant display. Like Raeff, he was a senior man who saw the young Mozart as a clever-clever young whippersnapper who needed the advice of his elders and betters. Dal Prato — 'my molto amato castrato Dal Prato', as Mozart called him, with loving exasperation — was, on the other hand, totally unburdened with experience, and he was not over-gifted with either talent or intelligence. Yet the big part of Idamante was his. The composer showed himself, not for the first time, as a kindly, skilled and patient teacher; he could take stupidity better than he could take conceit. As for the ladies, Dorothea and Elisabeth Wendling, they gave no trouble, God bless them, and they knew how to sing.

The first performance of *Idomeneo* took place on 29th January, 1781, two days after Mozart's birthday. His father and sister were present, and so we have no epistolary account of how things went.

15

In fact, we have very few records indeed of that premiere, and those that we have totally fail to mention the composer's name. Of the importance of the opera — despite inevitable faults, derived as much from Varesco's libretto as the composer's own comparative immaturity — posterity has no doubt.

Idomeneo is *seria,* lofty, statuesque, and yet human and warm. This is no place for a detailed musical analysis, and perhaps it is enough to affirm that the mere reading of the orchestral and vocal score is a hugely educative experience. The deployment of orchestral colour, the boldness and poignancy of the harmonies, the elevation of conventional 'tags' (like the cadence of Ilia's first recitative) into highly dramatic devices — these, and many more, aspects of the composition are a great wonder. But the totality — the balance of chorus and aria and ensemble, the sense of movement, the economy — reveals an architectonic genius which a mere symphony or concerto cannot always adequately show. And yet the strength of the work is a symphonic one, in which purely musical devices of contrast — wind against strings, chromatic anguish against diatonic assertiveness — are a counterpart, not a mere accompaniment, to the human drama.

Mozart went back to purely instrumental writing after the Munich premiere of *Idomeneo,* producing, for instance, the masterly Oboe Quartet. But creation cannot flourish without the means of subsistence, and Mozart was suffering from the jealousy and tight-fistedness of his Archbishop, who would not let his employee (whose genius he now certainly began to recognize) accept commissions or give performances outside the court, whether the court was in Salzburg or Vienna. Soon, after a blazing row with the proud prelate, Mozart left that servitude and tried to live as a free-lance teacher, composer and performer. Vienna became his centre, and it was here that he married Constanze Weber, the sister of Aloysia. He could be a fond husband and father but did not lose his artistic detachment: while his child was being born in one room he wrote his Quartet in D minor in the next. With a family to support, the need to raise money became a permanent obsession, and one means of raising it was the new device of the subscription concert. But debts always outgalloped income.

His output became, as we know, prodigious, and it raged over all the musical forms, not excluding opera — *Die Entführung aus dem Serail* (with a heroine named for his wife), which was produced at the Imperial Theatre, and the small but perfect *Der Schauspieldirektor*

16

for the imperial palace at Schönbrunn. But the next great operatic masterpiece was a marvel of *opera buffa* — *Le Nozze di Figaro*. The librettist for this was Lorenzo da Ponte, a half-Jew half-Gentile from Ceneda, north of Venice. His real name was Emanuele Conegliano, but, on his reception into the Catholic Church at the age of fourteen, he took the name of the officiating bishop. He was intended for the priesthood, 'though this', he said rightly, 'was utterly contrary to my vocation and my character.' But a seminary education made him skilful in Latin, including Latin versifying, and this proved no bad training for the managing of metre, as well as the compression of diction, in the Italian libretti which made his name. He became a somewhat dissolute priest, on the venerable Venetian model, and his profligacy, as well as his Rousseau-style rationalism, eventually led to his having to quit Venice.

Da Ponte was in Vienna in 1782, and in the following year he tried his hand at his first opera libretto, for the distinguished composer Salieri. A few years later, Mozart himself sought him out as a possible collaborator in a musical adaptation of Beaumarchais's *Le Mariage de Figaro*. The play itself had caused a scandal in Paris, because of its political implications (lost in the operatic version) — and it was banned in Vienna. Mozart foresaw no great difficulty in obtaining permission to produce a musical version, since music is supposed to draw the teeth of satire: the notoriety of the banned play would send the Viennese flocking to the unbanned opera.

There was some trouble with the libretto, both from the composer's point of view and the censor's, and it is hard to believe that, as Da Ponte was later to allege, the whole work was made ready for performance in six weeks. Indeed, of the background of the work we know little. We do know, however, that the first performance took place, at the command of the Emperor himself, on 1st May, 1786, and that the general response to it was very enthusiastic. Yet the public is always fickle, and it soon let *Figaro* be eclipsed by the work of a very indifferent composer, Vicente Martín y Soler, whose opera *Una Cosa Rara* was immensely popular but is not now well remembered. *Le Nozze di Figaro* only managed to secure a revival in Vienna when *Don Giovanni* brought Mozart back into prominence.

Mozart did not repine at the short-lived popularity of the work in Vienna, for there was another city — deservedly famous for its musical taste — that loved his stage-work and could not have enough of it. This was Prague. Mozart visited the Bohemian capital in 1787, at the invitation of his admirers, and Prague and he got on very well together: his keyboard improvisations on themes from *Figaro* brought the house down. The manager of the local Italian Opera, Pasquale Bondini, was especially delighted with Mozart, for *Figaro* had played to full houses all the winter of 1786-7 and much strengthened the normally precarious finances of his organization. He was quick, then, to commission a new opera for production the following winter, and Mozart went back to Vienna to consult with Da Ponte about a suitable subject.

Da Ponte was busy. He was writing *L'Arbore di Diana* for Martín and *Axur, Re d'Ormuz* for Salieri. All he could think of for Mozart was the story of Don Giovanni or Don Juan, already well-known and much used on the stage, and all he had time to do was to draw heavily on an existing libretto by Giovanni Bertati. Mozart probably started work at once, producing enough material to commence rehearsals. Then he took lodgings in Prague and got down to the rest of the opera. On 29 October 1787, he conducted the first performance, having − according to a legend that may not be true, merely *ben trovato* − completed the composition of the overture while the audience was still coming in. That audience acclaimed the work, and so did the audiences that crammed the theatre night after night thereafter, recognising it as a great dual triumph. Da Ponte, however much he owes his immortality to Mozart, showed that a libretto − even a derivative one − could be important art. And the words of Don Giovanni are exquisite − tender, witty, precise. Mozart could hardly fail to make a wonderful duet out of these lines:

DON GIOVANNI
Là ci darem la mano,
Là mi dirai di sì.
Vedi, non è lontano:
Partiam, ben mio, di qui.

ZERLINA
Vorrei, e non vorrei . . .
Mi trema un poco il cor . . .
Felice, è ver, sarei;
Ma può burlarmi ancor.

The story of Don Juan is an old one and appears to date back to a real, or mythical as opposed to literary, Spanish nobleman of Tenorio who was a noted profligate. Faust, Don Juan's cousin in sin, similarly derives from a personage real enough to be in the Acts of the Apostles — Simon Magus the Fortunate of Faustus. But, whereas the Faust story is one of the most terrible in Western culture, being the tale of a man who sells his soul for a few years of pleasure, the Don Juan legend has never seemed to be really tragic. Womanizers are admirable, pathetic, or comic, but — though they may deserve a thrashing on the bare buttocks in the Venetian manner — they are hardly hell-bait. And, if we look at the story closely, we will observe that Don Juan's being dragged to hell is only indirectly a punishment for his profligacy. His real crime is to insult the dead, which has traditionally been regarded as a terrible impiety with overtones of parricide about it. Thus, the Don Juan legend may be taken as a combination of two quite distinct stories, that of a man who lusts after women, and that of a man who wrongs the dead.

We need no particularized tale of philandering to produce a Don Juan image. Casanova — a real-life womanizer who actually, it is believed, helped with the preparation of *Don Giovanni* — will do for a great-lover myth, as will Frank Harris or Errol Flynn or even H.G. Wells. Don Juan has his place in the mythology of the West because of the manner of his blasphemy and his subsequent end. He kills a high hidalgo, the Commendador or Commendatore, who happens to be the father of one of his amatory victims, the Lady Anna. A statue is erected in honour of the great man, and Don Juan sneers at it. The statue comes to life (a very ancient, indeed classical, fabular device) and there is a supper invitation. In the opera, it is Don Giovanni who invites the Commendatore; in the older versions of the story it is the Commendador who invites Don Juan. The latter version is the more terrible and the more characteristic, since Don Juan is foolhardy enough to go to a graveyard where adders and other inedibles are served, and, as a *bonne bouche,* is dragged down to the city of the dead which lies beneath the gravestones. Da Ponte and Mozart were not really in search of terror, except in a Pickwickian sense. To them the legend is material for a kind of black comedy which is a new, and original, variant of *opera buffa.*

Da Ponte's predecessors in the field of dramatizing the legend are many and distinguished. We begin with Gabriel Tellez — or Tirso de Molina — in the early seventeenth century, whose *El Burlador de Sevilla* is not particularly distinguished (too much moralizing), though it contains many of the prototypes of Da Ponte's own characters. There are a Doña Anna and a Don Octavio — a decent

19

dull respectable lover — as well as a comic servant. In a mid-seventeenth-century Italian version of the story, put on at Naples, Harlequin took time off from the *Commedia dell'Arte* to act as Don Juan's servant, but the lineaments of Leporello can best be traced in Molière's *Le Festin de Pierre*, in 1665, where the servant is a well-rounded creation called Sganarelle. Moreover, Molière stresses the comic aspects of the story, dispensing with the hell-torments that were necessary to both Tirso de Molina and the Naples version. Here too are Donna Elvira, Masetto and Zerlina. Da Ponte obviously studied the play.

England took over the Don Juan theme a decade after Molière, with Shadwell's *The Libertine,* to which the divine Purcell contributed incidental music. In 1736, in Da Ponte's own Venice, Goldoni wrote a verse-play called *Don Giovanni Tenorio o sia il dissoluto,* less as an artistic venture than as an act of revenge on an actress — Signora Passalacqua — who had made a fool of him at the end of a protracted liaison. Don Giovanni would be recognized as his rival, Carino, the shepherd as himself, and the shepherdess Elsa as his former mistress. Here again, to judge from the similarity between Goldoni's last act and Da Ponte's finale, we seem to have another conscious source for the libretto. Finally, in 1775, came Bertati's version, the direct and immediate origin — not because of lack of inventive power on Da Ponte's part, solely because of lack of time — of the *Don Giovanni* that was the rage of Prague.

It is necessary for us to see the opera in relation to its time and to an existing stock of dramatic workings of the legend. Neither Mozart nor Da Ponte was drawn by inner artistic necessity to the theme: there was none of the sense of creating great art, like Goethe brooding for a long time on the Faust story and then pouring his life's blood into it. There was a theatrical commission to be fulfilled, and the Don Juan theme was the only one quickly available. Bondini in Prague wanted a new *Figaro,* so *Don Giovanni* had to be comic, not serious and moralistic. Fortunately, the Don Juan stage tradition had become a *buffo* one — from Molière on — so there would be no sense of wrenching an essentially grave theme into an unsuitable comic mould.

The singers available for *Don Giovanni* were those already engaged on *Figaro* when the new opera went into rehearsal. This limited Da Ponte as to characters (early versions of the story had a large number of personages — especially women, since Don Juan's profligacy had to be given arithmetical authenticity). Figaro steps easily into the role of Leporello. The tenor part in *Figaro* is not of great importance, so the tenor — Don Ottavio — of *Don Giovanni* has to be a minor role similarly suitable for a minor artist. Luigi Bassi, who sang the baritone part of the Count in *Figaro*, was a godsend of a villain-hero for the eponym of the new work — a fine actor, good-looking, only twenty-two. The three female parts of *Figaro* — all of roughly equal importance — are exactly matched in *Don Giovanni*. Mozart, considerate of his singers, always ready to cut his musical cloth to their vocal measure, reveals himself always as a pre-Beethoven artist — willing to change, omit, throw away whole sheets of glorious music in the service of expediency.

If the music had to be changed, the libretto too had to undergo modifications during rehearsal, and, in the absence of Da Ponte, recalled to Vienna for the first night of his and Martín's *L'Arbore,* it seems that Giacomo Casanova, whose qualifications were not just amatory, was called in to make delicate emendations. The libretto we have is surely perfect of its kind, strong in character interest, lucid and concise in language, and eminently singable. Based on myth. *Don Giovanni* has itself become a source of myth. The figures of the *Don Juan in Hell* in *Man and Superman* are essentially Shaw's but primarily Mozart's and Da Ponte's. When we think of Don Juan, it is not the *Burlador* or the self-projection of Byron that comes to mind but a comic villain with a fine baritone voice singing pithy Italian.

Of the felicities of the music it is needless, indeed impossible, to speak; music must always speak for itself. There is a trombone triumph. for the Commendatore, greater than that in Idomeneo, whose first intonations, says Shaw, represent a moment of dreadful joy for all musicians. The three orchestras in the ballroom, playing simultaneously in three different tempi, may have been primarily a tribute to the excellence of the Prague instrumentalists, who could cope with any ingenuity, but it is good drama in itself. And the final ensemble — too often omitted in performance, for it proclaims the essentially *buffo* character of a work that some, incredibly, would like to take for a serious morality — is a wonder of pseudo-profundity, a civilized grotesquerie to match the words:

> Resti dunque quel birbon
> Tra Proserpina e Pluton.

The rogue must dwell between Pluto and his queen for ever. Not the Christian inferno after all, but the stock classical Hades: three in a bed, Don Giovanni in the middle, but Pluto probably awake all the time. It is a pleasant conceit and a fitting punishment.

One of the results of the success of *Don Giovanni* was Mozart's elevation to Chamber Composer to the Emperor himself, but it was purely a nominal appointment and did nothing to ease circumstances that — however much music he wrote — were destined to remain wretched till the end of his life. He had no money sense, nor did his wife, and it is painful to think of the poverty, partly self-induced, that is the background to the last three great symphonies, written in a single summer, that came after *Don Giovanni*. But, besides Mozart's own improvidence, we have to remember that the system of royalties, which keeps today's composers alive, did not then exist, and that the outright fee paid for a commission was never exactly princely, even though a prince sometimes paid it. Many of Mozart's final letters are begging letters, requests for loans that, he assures his correspondents, will be repaid when the present 'temporary embarrassment' is over. But the embarrassments grew into one permanent embarrassment, and led to a pauper's grave. Mozart died in 1791. He was only thirty-five.

Perhaps it is worth dying young and in poverty if one can produce — among other masterpieces — an *Idomeneo* and a *Don Giovanni*. But we listeners to these works, entranced and elevated, ought occasionally to allow ourselves the luxury of anger. In Mozart's own works there is neither anger nor self-pity, only humour, elegance and a nobility sometimes — though always impersonally — tragic. His music contains the image of a perfectly ordered civilization which is itself an image of divine order.

ANTHONY BURGESS

DON GIOVANNI

Libretto by Lorenzo da Ponte

DRAMATIS PERSONAE

DON GIOVANNI, *an extremely licentious young nobleman*
DONNA ANNA, *promised in marriage to*
DON OTTAVIO
THE COMMENDATORE, *father of Donna Anna*
DONNA ELVIRA, *a woman of Burgos, deserted by Don Giovanni*
LEPORELLO, *Don Giovanni's servant*
MASETTO, *a peasant, betrothed to*
ZERLINA

Chorus of peasants, servants, etc.

The opera is set in a Spanish city, traditionally Seville.

24

Synopsis

ACT I

Outside the Commendatore's house, at night. A mutinous Leporello awaits his master, who is attempting to seduce Donna Anna. She appears, struggling desperately with the masked Don Giovanni, and as she runs to fetch help, her father enters. The old man challenges Don Giovanni to fight, and is killed. The Don and Leporello escape. Donna Anna returns with Don Ottavio, and, over-wrought by the sight of her father's corpse, makes Don Ottavio swear to avenge his death.

A street, at dawn. Leporello complains half-heartedly at the life Don Giovanni is leading, but both retire at the approach of an unknown woman. It is Donna Elvira, who has arrived in search of Don Giovanni. As he approaches her, she recognizes and reproaches him, but he manages to escape, leaving Leporello to torment her with the list of his other conquests.

Open country, with Don Giovanni's palace in the background. Zerlina and Masetto, and their friends, joyfully celebrate their forthcoming marriage. The Don comes upon them and instructs Leporello to conduct the company, including a most unwilling Masetto, to his palace for entertainment. Zerlina alone remains but Don Giovanni's seduction of her is thwarted by Donna Elvira, who triumphantly leads the girl away. Donna Anna and Don Ottavio enter, and are about to seek Don Giovanni's aid when Donna Elvira re-appears and accuses him of treachery and falsehood. Don Giovanni tries to pass her off as mad, but their suspicions are aroused, and the intonation of his parting words convinces Donna Anna that he is indeed her father's killer. She reminds Don Ottavio of his oath, but he finds it hard to accept the truth of her accusation. After they have left, Leporello reports his success in getting rid of Donna Elvira whilst keeping Zerlina in the palace, and Don Giovanni orders him to prepare the evening's festivities.

That evening outside the Don's palace. Masetto chides Zerlina for her supposed faithlessness, but both are led into the palace. Donna Anna, Donna Elvira and Don Ottavio enter, masked, and are invited to join the festivities.

The ballroom. At the height of the dancing, Zerlina's cries for help are heard.

Don Giovanni tries to put the blame on Leporello, but Donna Anna, Donna Elvira and Don Ottavio unmask and confront him. Master and servant escape.

ACT II

A street outside Donna Elvira's house, at night. In the face of further protests from Leporello about his way of life. the Don orders him to exchange clothes so that he may the better lay siege to Donna Elvira's maid. Elvira appears on the balcony, and Don Giovanni feigns repentance from underneath. She descends, supposes the disguised Leporello to be Don Giovanni, and goes off with him. The Don's serenading of the maid is interrupted by a posse of heavily armed peasants led by Masetto in search of Zerlina's attacker. In the person of Leporello, Don Giovanni sends them on a wild goose chase and then sets about Masetto before disappearing into the darkness.

A courtyard in Donna Anna's house. Leporello, trying to get rid of Donna Elvira, is trapped by Donna Anna, Don Ottavio, Masetto and Zerlina. He is forced to reveal himself, much to Donna Elvira's humiliation, and then manages to escape. Convinced now of Don Giovanni's guilt, Don Ottavio prepares to inform the authorities.

A walled cemetery. Don Giovanni and Leporello compare notes on their various escapades, and are interrupted by a threatening voice from the marble monument on the Commendatore's tomb. The reckless Don forces the terrified Leporello to invite the statue to supper. The statue nods assent.

A room in Donna Anna's house. Confident that Don Giovanni will not long remain unpunished, Don Ottavio urges Donna Anna to marry him. She pleads too great sorrow, but re-affirms her love.

The grand hall of Don Giovanni's palace. The Don is at supper, served by Leporello. Donna Elvira bursts in and implores him for the last time to mend his ways. Rebuffed, she leaves, and her screams herald the arrival of the stone guest. The statue bids Don Giovanni repent, but proudly obstinate to the last he refuses and the tortures of the damned commence. The rest of the cast enter in search of him, and Leporello describes his descent into hell. They join in pointing the moral direct to the audience.

Atto primo

Act one

SCENA PRIMA

SCENE 1

Giardino – Notte. Leporello, con ferraiolo, passeggia davanti alla casa di Donna Anna; indi Don Giovanni e Donna Anna ed in ultimo il Commendatore.
Leporello entra dal lato destro con lanterna in mano.

A garden. Night. Leporello, in a cloak, is pacing up and down in front of Donna Anna's house; later Don Giovanni and Donna Anna and finally the Commendatore.
Leporello enters from the right with a lantern in his hand.

1. INTRODUZIONE

1. INTRODUCTION

LEPORELLO
Notte e giorno faticar
per chi nulla sa gradir;
pioggia e vento sopportar,
mangiar male e mal dormir!
Voglio fare il gentiluomo,
e non voglio più servir.
Oh, che caro galantuomo!
Vuol star dentro con la bella,
ed io far la sentinella!
Voglio fare il gentiluomo,
e non voglio più servir.
Ma mi par che venga gente . . .
Non mi voglio far sentir.

LEPORELLO
Slaving night and day
for one whom nothing pleases,
enduring rain and wind,
ill fed and short of sleep!
I'd like to live the life of a gentleman
and serve no more.
Oh, what a fine gallant!
He like to be indoors with a beauty
while I keep watch outside!
I'd like to live the life of a gentleman
and serve no more.
But I think someone's coming . . .
I don't wish to be seen.

(si ritira)

(he withdraws)

Don Giovanni esce dal palazzo del Commendatore inseguito da Donna Anna; cerca coprirsi il viso ed è avvolto in un lungo mantello.

Don Giovanni comes out of the Commendatore's house followed by Donna Anna; he is trying to hide his face and is wrapped in a long mantle.

ANNA
(trattenendo Don Giovanni)
Non sperar, se non m'uccidi,
ch'io ti lasci fuggir mai.

GIOVANNI
(sempre cercando di celarsi)
Donna folle! indarno gridi;
chi son io tu non saprai.

LEPORELLO
(avanzandosi; tra sé)
Che tumulto! O ciel; che gridi!
Il padron in nuovi guai!

ANNA
Gente! servi! al traditore!

GIOVANNI
Taci, e trema al mio furore!

ANNA
Scellerato!

GIOVANNI
Sconsigliata!
(tra sé)
Questa furia disperata
mir vuol far precipitar.

ANNA
Come furia disperata
ti saprò perseguitar.

LEPORELLO
(tra sé)
Sta a veder che il malandrino
mi farà precipitar.

COMMENDATORE
(con spada e lume)
Lasciala, indegno!
Battiti meco!

*(Donna Anna, udendo la voce del
padre, lascia Don Giovanni ed
entra in casa)*

ANNA
(holding Don Giovanni back)
Unless you kill me, you need not hope
I'll ever let you escape.

GIOVANNI
(still trying to conceal himself)
Crazy woman! you cry out in vain:
you shall not know who I am.

LEPORELLO
(coming forward; aside)
What a din! Heavens, what an uproar!
Master's in trouble again!

ANNA
Help me, someone! Seize the traitor!

GIOVANNI
Hold your peace, or fear my rage.

ANNA
Vile monster!

GIOVANNI
She's raving!
(aside)
This wild Fury
will bring about my downfall.

ANNA
Like an avenging Fury
I'll pursue you ever.

LEPORELLO
(aside)
You'll see the rascal
will leave me to foot the bill.

COMMENDATORE
(carrying a sword and a lamp)
Unhand her, villain!
Draw and defend yourself!

*(Donna Anna, hearing her father's
voice, releases Don Giovanni and
goes into the house)*

GIOVANNI
Va! non mi degno
di pugnar teco.

GIOVANNI
Away! it would not be proper
for me to fight you.

COMMENDATORE
Così pretendi da me fuggir?

COMMENDATORE
You think to escape me thus?

LEPORELLO
(tra sé)
Potessi almeno di qua partir!

LEPORELLO
(aside)
If I could only get away somehow!

GIOVANNI
Misero! attendi
se vuoi morir.

GIOVANNI
Poor fool! stay then,
if you really wish to die.

*(Si battono. Il Commendatore
è mortalmente ferito)*

*(They fight. The Commendatore is
mortally wounded)*

COMMENDATORE
Ah, soccorso! son tradito . . .
L'assassino m'ha ferito . . .
e dal seno palpitante
sento l'anima partir . . .

COMMENDATORE
Help! I am undone! . . .
The assassin's blade has pierced me . . .
and from my throbbing breast
I feel my life ebb away . . .

GIOVANNI
(tra sé)
Ah! già cade il sciagurato
Affannosa e agonizzante
già dal seno palpitante
veggo l'anima partir.

GIOVANNI
(aside)
The rash old man is down . . .
in mortal agony he lies;
I see his life ebbing away
from his throbbing breast.

(Il Commendatore muore)

(The Commendatore dies)

LEPORELLO
(tra sé)
Qual misfatto! qual eccesso!
Entro il sen, dallo spavento,
palpitar il cor mi sento.
Io non so che far, che dir.

LEPORELLO
(aside)
How appalling! There's been murder!
I can feel my heart
pounding with terror in my breast.
I don't know what to do or say.

SCENA SECONDA

SCENE 2

Don Giovanni e Leporello

Don Giovanni and Leporello

RECITATIVO

RECITATIVE

GIOVANNI
(sotto voce)
Leporello, ove sei?

GIOVANNI
(sotto voce)
Leporello, where are you?

LEPORELLO
Son qui, per mia disgrazia. E voi?

GIOVANNI
Son qui.

LEPORELLO
Chi è morto? voi o il vecchio?

GIOVANNI
Che domanda da bestia! Il vecchio.

LEPORELLO
Bravo! Due imprese leggiadre;
sforzar la figlia, ed ammazzar
il padre.

GIOVANNI
L'ha voluto: suo danno.

LEPORELLO
Ma Donna Anna, cos'ha voluto!

GIOVANNI
Taci, non mi seccar. Vien meco,
(in atto di batterlo)
se non vuoi qualche
cosa ancor tu.

LEPORELLO
Non vo'nulla, signor;
non parlo più.

*(alzando da terra la lanterna ed il
mantello. Partono)*

SCENA TERZA

*Don Ottavio, Donna Anna e
Servi con lumi*

ANNA
Ah! del padre in periglio
in soccorso voliam!

OTTAVIO
(con ferro ignudo in mano)
Tutto il mio sangue
verserò, se bisogna;
ma dov'è il scellerato?

LEPORELLO
I'm here, worse luck. And you, sir?

GIOVANNI
I'm here.

LEPORELLO
Who's dead? You or the old man?

GIOVANNI
What an idiotic question! The old man.

LEPORELLO
Well done! Two pretty exploits:
to ravish the girl and butcher
her father.

GIOVANNI
It's his fault: he would have it so.

LEPORELLO
And Donna Anna . . . Would she have it so

GIOVANNI
Silence! Don't provoke me. Come along,
(threateningly)
unless you want me to give you
something for yourself.

LEPORELLO
I want nothing, sir:
I'll not say another word.

*(picking up the lantern and
cloak. Exeunt)*

SCENE 3

*Don Ottavio, Donna Anna and
servants with lights*

ANNA
Come, my father's in danger;
we must hasten to his aid!

OTTAVIO
(with a drawn sword in his hand)
I'll shed all my life-blood,
if need be;
but where is the ruffian?

ANNA
In questo loco

(vede il cadavere)

2. RECITATIVO E DUETTO

ANNA
Ma qual mai s'offre, o Dei,
spettacolo funesto agli occhi miei!
Il padre! padre mio! mio caro padre!

OTTAVIO
Signore . . .

ANNA
Ah! l'assassino
mel trucidò. Quel sangue,
quella piaga, quel volto
tinto e coperto del color di morte.
Ei non respira più . . .
fredde ha le membra . . .
Padre mio! caro padre! padre amato!
Io manco . . . io moro.

(sviene)

OTTAVIO
Ah! soccorrete, amici, il mio tesoro!
Cercatemi, recatemi qualche odor,
qualche spirto. Ah! non tardate!

(Partono due servi)

Donna Anna! sposa! amica!
Il duolo estremo
la meschinella uccide!

ANNA
Ahi!

(Ritornano i servi)

OTTAVIO
Già rinviene.
Datele nuovi aiuti.

ANNA
Padre mio!

ANNA
This was the place.

(she sees the body)

2. RECITATIVE AND DUET

ANNA
But . . . O God, what dreadful sight
confronts my eyes!
Father! my father! dearest father!

OTTAVIO
Dear sir . . .

ANNA
Ah! the assassin
has struck him down! This blood . . .
this wound . . . his face
discoloured with the pallor of death.
He is not breathing . . .
his limbs are cold.
Oh father, dear father, dearest father!
I'm fainting . . . I'm dying.

(she faints)

OTTAVIO
Quick, friends, help my dear one!
Find some scent, bring some spirits . . .
do not delay!

(Two servants hurry out)

Donna Anna! my dearest! beloved! . . .
Her great sorrow
has killed her!

ANNA
Ah!

(The servants return)

OTTAVIO
She's reviving:
give her more assistance.

ANNA
My father!

OTTAVIO
Celate, allontanate agli occhi suoi
quell'oggetto d'orrore.
(Viene portato via il cadavere)
Anima mia, consolati, fa core!

(DUETTO)

ANNA
Fuggi, crudele, fuggi!
Lascia che mora anch'io
ora ch'è morto, oh Dio!
chi a me la vita dié.

OTTAVIO
Senti, cor mio, deh! senti:
guardami un solo istante;
ti parla il caro amante
che vive sol per te.

ANNA
Tu sei! perdon, mio bene . . .
L'affanno mio . . . le pene . . .
Ah! il padre mio dov'è?

OTTAVIO
Il padre . . . lascia, o cara,
la rimembranza amara:
hai sposo e padre in me.

ANNA
Ah! vendicar, se il puoi,
giura quel sangue ognor.

OTTAVIO
Lo giuro agli occhi tuoi,
lo giuro al nostro amor.

ANNA ED OTTAVIO
Che giuramento, oh Dei!
Che barbaro momento!
Tra cento affetti e cento
vammi ondeggiando il cor.

(partono)

OTTAVIO
Bear away this fearful victim
from out her sight.
(The body is carried out)
Beloved, be comforted, take courage!

(DUET)

ANNA
Leave me, cruel one, leave me!
Let me die too, O God,
now he who gave me life
is dead.

OTTAVIO
Hear me, dearest, hear me;
look at me but for a moment;
this is your true love here,
who lives for you alone.

ANNA
You live! Forgive me, dear . . .
My grief, my distress . . .
Oh my father, where is he?

OTTAVIO
Your father? Dearest, do not dwell
on that bitter memory:
you have both betrothed and father in me

ANNA
Swear that, if you can,
you will avenge his blood!

OTTAVIO
I swear it by your eyes,
I swear it by our love.

BOTH
O solemn oath
in this dread moment!
A thousand painful emotions
jostle in my heart.

(exeunt)

SCENA QUARTA

Strada. Alba Chiara.
Don Giovanni e Leporello, poi
Donna Elvira in abito da viaggio.

RECITATIVO

GIOVANNI
Orsù, spicciati presto. Cosa vuoi?

LEPORELLO
L'affar di cui si tratta è importante.

GIOVANNI
Lo credo.

LEPORELLO
È importantissimo.

GIOVANNI
Meglio ancora! Finiscila.

LEPORELLO
Giurate di non andar in collera.

GIOVANNI
Lo giuro sul mio onore,
purché non parli del Commendatore.

LEPORELLO
Siamo soli?

GIOVANNI
Lo vedo.

LEPORELLO
Nessun ci sente?

GIOVANNI
Via.

LEPORELLO
Vi posso dire tutto liberamente? ...

GIOVANNI
Sì.

SCENE 4

A street. Dawn.
Don Giovanni and Leporello, then
Donna Elvira in travelling clothes

RECITATIVE

GIOVANNI
Well now, quickly! What is it you want?

LEPORELLO
Sir, it's a matter of importance.

GIOVANNI
Well then . . .

LEPORELLO
Of the greatest importance.

GIOVANNI
Better still! Out with it!

LEPORELLO
Promise you won't fly into a rage.

GIOVANNI
I promise on my honour, so long
as you don't mention the Commendatore.

LEPORELLO
Are we alone?

GIOVANNI
It seems so.

LEPORELLO
No one can hear?

GIOVANNI
Go on, man!

LEPORELLO
I can speak out quite freely?

GIOVANNI
Yes.

LEPORELLO
Dunque, quand'è così,
caro signor padrone,
(all'orecchio, ma forte)
la vita che menate é da briccone.

GIOVANNI
Temerario! in tal guisa . . .

LEPORELLO
E il giuramento?

GIOVANNI
Non so di giuramento.
Taci, o ch'io . . .

LEPORELLO
Non parlo più, non fiato,
o padron mio.

GIOVANNI
Così saremo amici. Or odi un poco:
sai tu perché son qui?

LEPORELLO
Non ne so nulla.
Ma, essendo l'alba chiara, non
sarebbe qualche nuova conquista?
Io lo devo saper per porla in lista.

GIOVANNI
Va là, che se'il grand'uom! Sappi
ch'io sono innamorato d'una bella
dama, e son certo che m'ama.
La vidi, le parlai; meco al casino
questa notte verrà.
Zitto: mi pare
sentir odor di femmina . . .

(Viene dal fondo Donna Elvira)

LEPORELLO
(tra sé)
Cospetto! Che odorato perfetto!

GIOVANNI
All'aria mi par bella.

LEPORELLO
(tra sé)
E che occhio, dico!

34

LEPORELLO
Well then, this is it,
my dear lord and master:
(shouting in his ear)
you're leading the life of a scoundrel!

GIOVANNI
Impudent rascal! How dare you . . .

LEPORELLO
You gave your promise, sir!

GIOVANNI
I recall no promise.
Be silent, or I'll . . .

LEPORELLO
I'll not say another word, sir,
not another whisper.

GIOVANNI
Then we can be friends again. Now listen
to me: do you know why I'm here?

LEPORELLO
I don't know at all;
but at this late hour, won't
it be some new conquest?
I should know who, so as to list her.

GIOVANNI
If you aren't the great man!
Know then that I'm enamoured
of a lovely lady,
and I'm sure she loves me too.
I saw her, I addressed her;
tonight she is to come to my villa.
But hush! I scent a woman's presence.

(Donna Elvira enters from the rear)

LEPORELLO
(aside)
Heavens, what an expert sense of smell!

GIOVANNA
She seems pretty, too.

LEPORELLO
(aside)
And what an eye, as well!

GIOVANNI
Ritiriamoci un poco,
e scopriamo terren.

GIOVANNI
Let's step aside a moment
and spy out the land.

LEPORELLO
(tra sé)
Già prese foco.

LEPORELLO
(aside)
He's on fire already!

(vanno in disparte)

(they withdraw)

SCENA QUINTA

Donna Elvira e detti

SCENE 5

Donna Elvira and the above

3. ARIA E TERZETTO

3. ARIA AND TRIO

ELVIRA
Ah! chi mi dice mai
quel barbaro dov'è,
che per mio scorno amai,
che mi mancò di fé?
Ah! se ritrovo l'empio,
e a me non torna ancor,
vo' farne orrendo scempio,
gli vo' cavare il cor.

ELVIRA
O who can tell me now
where is the knave
whom, to my shame, I loved,
and who betrayed my trust?
Ah! if I find the traitor
and he will not return to me,
I'll kill him most horribly
and tear out his heart.

GIOVANNI
(piano a Leporello)
Udisti? qualche bella
dal vago abbandonata . . . Poverina!
Cerchiam di consolare il suo
tormento.

GIOVANNI
(softly, to Leporello)
You heard that? A damsel
deserted by her lover . . . Poor girl!
Let's attempt to console her in her
sorrow.

LEPORELLO
(tra sé)
Così ne consolò milleottocento.

LEPORELLO
(aside)
As he's consoled some eighteen hundred.

GIOVANNI
Signorina . . .

GIOVANNI
Dear young lady . . .

RECITATIVO

RECITATIVE

ELVIRA
Chi è là?

ELVIRA
Who's there?

GIOVANNI
Stelle! che vedo!

GIOVANNI
Heavens! Whom do I see?

LEPORELLO
(tra sé)
Oh bella! Donna Elvira!

ELVIRA
Don Giovanni! . . .
Sei qui, mostro, fellon,
nido d'inganni? . . .

LEPORELLO
(tra sé)
Che titoli cruscanti! Manco male
che lo conosce bene!

GIOVANNI
Via, cara Donna Elvira,
Calmate quella collera . . . sentite.
Lasciatemi parlar . . .

ELVIRA
Cosa puoi dire,
dopo azion si nera? In casa mia
entri furtivamente. A forza d'arte,
di giuramenti e di lusinghe, arrivi
a sedurre il cor mio:
m'innamori, o crudele!
Mi dichiari tua sposa.
E poi, mancando
della terra e del ciel al santo dritto,
con enorme delitto
dopo tre di da Burgos t'allontani.
M'abbandoni, mi fuggi,
e lasci in preda
al rimorso ed al pianto
per pena forse che t'amai cotanto!

LEPORELLO
(tra sé)
Pare un libro stampato!

GIOVANNI
Oh! In quanto a questo ebbi le mie
ragioni!
(a Leporello, ironicamente)
È vero?

LEPORELLO
È vero. E che ragioni forti!

ELVIRA
E quali sono,

LEPORELLO
(aside)
Delightful! Donna Elvira!

ELVIRA
Don Giovanni! . . .
You here, you monster of vice,
you arch-deceiver?

LEPORELLO
(aside)
High-flown titles! All the better,
since she really knows him!

GIOVANNI
Come, dear Donna, Elvira,
calm yourself . . . listen . . .
let me speak.

ELVIRA
What can you say
after such baseness?
You stole into my house:
with fair words; vows and flattery
you succeeded in seducing my affections:
you gained my love, cruel one!
You declared me your wife.
And then, casting aside
the most sacred tie of earth and heaven
— o monstrous villain! — three days later
you went away from Burgos.
You left me forsaken, a prey to remorse
and bitter weeping:
was it a judgement for having
loved too much?

LEPORELLO
(aside)
She talks like a novel!

GIOVANNI
Oh, for all this I had my
reasons.
(to Leporello, ironically)
Hadn't I?

LEPORELLO
You had; and very important reasons!

ELVIRA
And what are they,

se non la tua perfidia,
la leggerezza tua? Ma il giusto cielo
volle ch'io ti trovassi
per far le sue, le mie vendette.

GIOVANNI
Eh, via! Siate più ragionevole.
(tra sé)
Mi pone a cimento costei.
(a Donna Elvira)
Se non credete al labbro mio,·
credete a questo galantuomo.

LEPORELLO
(tra sé)
Salvo il vero.

GIOVANNI
(forte)
Via, dille un poco.

LEPORELLO
(sotto voce a Don Giovanni)
E cosa devo dirle?

GIOVANNI
Sì, sì, dille pur tutto.
(parte non visto da Donna Elvira)

ELVIRA
Ebben, fa presto.

LEPORELLO
(balbettando)
Madama . . . veramente . . .
in questo mondo
conciossiacosaquandofosseché . . .
il quadro non è tondo . . .

ELVIRA
Sciagurato!
Così del mio dolor gioco ti prendi?
Ah! voi! . . .
*(verso Don Giovanni che non
crede partito)*
Stelle! l'iniquo fuggì!
misera me! Dov'è? in qual parte?

LEPORELLO
Eh! lasciate che vada. Egli non
merta che di lui ci pensiate.

if not your treachery and profligacy?
But it was Heaven's will
that I should find you,
to be its instrument of vengeance.

GIOVANNI
Come, come, do be reasonable . . .
(aside)
This woman's driving me crazy.
(to Donna Elvira)
If you won't believe what I say,
at least believe this honest fellow.

LEPORELLO
(aside)
Thank you kindly.

GIOVANNI
(aloud)
Well, tell her then.

LEPORELLO
(sotto voce to Don Giovanni)
But what am I to tell her?

GIOVANNI
Oh, tell her everything.
(exit unseen by Donna Elvira)

ELVIRA
Well now, make haste.

LEPORELLO
(stammering)
Madam . . . to tell the truth . . . in this
world, you know, the fact is
in a manner of speaking, as it were,
a square is different from a circle . . .

ELVIRA
Wretch!
Would you mock my grief?
And you! . . .
*(towards Don Giovanni, not
knowing him gone)*
Oh heaven! the villain's fled!
Woe is me! Where is he? Was it this way?

LEPORELLO
Oh, let him go: he's not worth
your thought.

37

ELVIRA
Lo scellerato m'ingannò,
mi tradì . . .

LEPORELLO
Eh! consolatevi;
non siete voi, non foste e non sarete
né la prima, né l'ultima. Guardate:
questo non picciol libro è tutto pieno
de' nomi di sue belle;
(cava di tasca una lista)
ogni villa, ogni borgo, ogni paese
è testimon di sue donnesche imprese.

4. ARIA

LEPORELLO
Madamina, il catalogo è questo.
delle belle che amò il padron mio:
un catalogo egli è che ho fatt'io;
osservate, leggete con me.
In Italia seicentoquaranta,
in Almagna duecentotrentuna,
cento in Francia, in Turchia
novantuna, ma in Ispagna son
già mille e tre.
V'han fra queste contadine,
cameriere, cittadine,
v'han contesse, baronesse,
marchesine, principesse,
e v'han donne d'ogni grado,
d'ogni forma, d'ogni età.

Nella bionda egli ha l'usanza
di lodar la gentilezza;
nella bruna, la costanza;
nella bianca, la dolcezza;
vuol d'inverno la grassotta,
vuol d'estate la magrotta;
è la grande maestosa,
la piccina è ognor vezzosa;
delle vecchie fa conquista
pel piacer di porle in lista,
Ma passion predominante
è la giovin principiante;
non si picca se sia ricca,
se sia brutta, se sia bella;
purché porti la gonnella,
voi sapete quel che fa.

(parte)

ELVIRA
But the scoundrel deceived me,
betrayed me . . .

LEPORELLO
Well, console yourself;
for you neither are, nor were, nor will be,
the first or the last of them.
Look at this sizeable volume;
it's full of the names of his conquests.
(takes a list from a pocket)
Every village, every town, every country
bears witness to his amorous adventures.

4. ARIA

LEPORELLO
Little lady, this is the list
of the beauties my master has courted,
a list I've made out myself:
take a look, read it with me.
In Italy six hundred and forty,
in Germany two hundred and thirty-one,
a hundred in France, ninety-one in
Turkey; but in Spain already a thousand
and three.
Some you see are country girls,
waiting maids, city beauties,
some are countesses, baronesses,
marchionesses, princesses:
women of every rank,
of every size, of every age.

He will praise
a fair girl's kindness,
a dark one's constancy,
a white-haired one's sweetness;
in winter he prefers them plump,
in summer slim;
he calls a tall one stately,
a tiny one always dainty.
Even the elderly he courts
for the pleasure of adding her to the list;
but his supreme passion
is the young beginner.
He cares not if she's poor or rich,
plain or pretty —
so long as she wears a skirt,
you know what his game is!

(exit)

38

SCENA SESTA	SCENE 6

Donna Elvira sola   *Donna Elvira alone*

RECITATIVO   RECITATIVE

ELVIRA
In questa forma dunque
mi tradì il scellerato!
È questo il premio che quel
barbaro rende all'amor mio?
Ah! vendicar vogl'io l'ingannato
mio cor. Pria ch'ei mi fugga
si ricorra . . . si vada . . .
Io sento in petto
sol vendetta parlar, rabbia e dispetto.

ELVIRA
This then is how the scoundrel
betrayed me!
Is this the reward
the ingrate gives me for my love?
I'll be revenged on my heart's deceiver.
Before he escapes me I'll call . . .
I'll go . . . In my heart
I hear the voice only
of vengeance, rage and indignation.

(parte)   *(exit)*

SCENA SETTIMA	SCENE 7

*Paese contiguo al palazzo di
Don Giovanni.
Zerlina, Masetto e Coro di
Contadina d'ambo i sessi, che
cantano, suonano e ballano*

*Countryside close to Don Giovanni's
palace.
Zerlina, Masetto and chorus of
villagers of both sexes, singing,
playing and dancing*

5. DUETTO E CORO   5. DUET AND CHORUS

ZERLINA
Giovinette, che fate all'amore,
non lasciate che passi l'età;
se nel seno vi bulica il core,
il rimedio vedetelo qua.
La ra la, la ra la, la ra la.
Che piacer! che piacer che sarà!

ZERLINA
You maidens whose thoughts dwell
on love, don't let time pass you by;
if your hearts are on fire within you,
you see the remedy here.
La ra la, la ra la, la ra la.
What pleasure, what pleasure in store!

CORO
La ra la . . .

CHORUS
La ra la . . .

MASETTO
Giovinetti, leggeri di testa,
non andate girando qua a là;
poco dura de' matti la festa,
ma per me cominciato non ha.
La ra la, la ra la, la ra la.
Che piacer! che piacer che sarà!

MASETTO
Giddy youths,
give up your trifling;
the fun of your dalliance soon passes,
for me it's scarcely begun.
La ra la, la ra la, la ra la.
What pleasure, what pleasure in store!

CORO
La ra la . . .

CHORUS
La ra la . . .

ZERLINA E MASETTO
Vieni, vieni, carino (a), godiamo,
e cantiamo, e balliamo, e suoniamo.
Vieni, vieni, carino (a), godiamo,
che piacer! che piacer che sarà!

ZERLINA AND MASETTO
Come, my dearest, rejoice,
let's dance and let's sing.
Come, my dearest, rejoice:
what pleasure, what pleasure in store!

SCENA OTTAVA

Don Giovanni, Leporello e detti

RECITATIVO

SCENE 8

Don Giovanni, Leporello and the above

RECITATIVE

GIOVANNI
Manco male, è partita . . .
(Da parte, a Leporello)
Oh guarda, guarda che bella gioventù,
che belle donne!

GIOVANNI
She's gone, thank the Lord . . .
(aside to Leporello)
But look, just look at those young people:
what pretty girls!

LEPORELLO
(tra sé)
Fra tante, per mia fe,
vi sarà qualche cosa anche per me.

LEPORELLO
(aside)
Upon my word, among so many
there may be something for me too.

GIOVANNI
Cari amici, buon giorno.
Seguitate a stare allegramente;
seguitate a suonar, o brava gente.
C'è qualche sposalizio?

GIOVANNI
Good day, dear friends!
Do not interrupt your merry-making:
continue with your singing, I pray you.
Is this a wedding party?

ZERLINA
Si, signore, e la sposa son io.

ZERLINA
Yes, sir, and I'm the bride.

GIOVANNI
Me ne consolo. Lo sposo?

GIOVANNI
I'm delighted. Who's the groom?

MASETTO
Io, per servirla.

MASETTO
Here, at your service.

GIOVANNI
Oh, bravo! per servirmi
questo è vero parlar da galantuomo.

GIOVANNI
Excellent! At my service!
Spoken like a gentleman.

LEPORELLO
(tra sè)
Basta che sia marito!

LEPORELLO
(aside)
Enough that he's the husband!

ZERLINA
Oh! il mio Masetto
è un uom d'ottimo core.

ZERLINA
Oh, my Masetto's
the kindest-hearted man.

40

GIOVANNI
Oh, anch'io, vedete!
Voglio che siamo amici.
Il vostro nome?

GIOVANNI
And so am I, my dear!
We must be friends.
What is your name?

ZERLINA
Zerlina.

ZERLINA
Zerlina.

GIOVANNI
(a Masetto)
E il tuo?

GIOVANNI
to Masetto)
And yours?

MASETTO
Masetto.

MASETTO
Masetto.

GIOVANNI
Oh! caro il mio Masetto!
Cara la mia Zerlina! V'esibisco
la mia protezïone... Leporello?...
*(a Leporello che fa scherzi alle
altre contadine)*
Cosa fai lì, birbone?

GIOVANNI
My dear Masetto!
My dear Zerlina!
I offer you my protection...
*(to Leporello, who is joking with
some of the girls)*
Leporello! What are you doing, rascal?

LEPORELLO
Anch'io, caro padrone,
esibisco la mia protezïone.

LEPORELLO
I too, worthy master,
am offering my protection.

GIOVANNI
Presto; va con costor: nel mio
palazzo conducili sul fatto:
ordina che abbiano cioccolata,
caffè, vini, prosciutti:
cerca divertir tutti,
mostra loro il giardino,
la galleria, le camere: in effetto
*(nel passare vicino a Zerlina la
prende par la vita)*
fa che resti contento il mio Masetto.
Hai capito?

GIOVANNI
Well, go with them: conduct them
at once to my palace.
Order them chocolate, coffee, wines,
refreshments;
see they are all entertained;
show them the garden,
the pictures, the apartments.
*(as he passes by Zerlina he takes her
round the waist)*
Take special care of my friend Masetto.
You understand me?

LEPORELLO
Ho capito. Andiam.

LEPORELLO
I understand you. Come along!

MASETTO
Signore...

MASETTO
But sir...

GIOVANNI
Cosa c'è?

GIOVANNI
What is it?

MASETTO
La Zerlina senza me non può star.

MASETTO
Zerlina can't stay here without me.

41

LEPORELLO
(a Masetto)
In vostro loco
ci sarà sua eccellenza, e saprà bene
fare le vostre parti.

GIOVANNI
Oh! la Zerlina
è in man d'un cavalier. Va pur;
fra poco ella meco verrà.

ZERLINA
Va, non temere;
nelle mani son io d'un cavaliere.

MASETTO
E per questo . . .

ZERLINA
E per questo non c'è da dubitar . . .

MASETTO
Ed io, cospetto!

GIOVANNI
Olà, finiam le dispute;
se subito, senz'altro replicar,
non te ne vai,
(mostrandogli la spada)
Masetto, guarda ben, ti pentirai.

6. ARIA

MASETTO
(a Don Giovanni)
Ho capito, signor sì!
Chino il capo e me ne vo;
già che piace a voi così,
altre repliche non fo.
Cavalier voi siete già,
dubitar non posso, affé;
me lo dice la bontà
che volete aver per me.
(a Zerlina, a parte)
Bricconaccia, malandrina,
fosti ognor la mia ruina.
*(a Leporello che lo vuol
condur seco)*
Vengo, vengo!
(a Zerlina)
Resta, resta!

LEPORELLO
to Masetto)
His lordship
will be here in your stead,
and he's well able to take your place.

GIOVANNI
Zerlina's in a gentleman's hands.
Go on: you'll see her
with me soon.

ZERLINA
Yes, don't be afraid;
I'm in a gentleman's hands.

MASETTO
And so . . .

ZERLINA
And so you need have no doubts.

MASETTO
Indeed, I haven't!

GIOVANNI
Come, let's have done with squabbling!
I tell you, Masetto, if you don't go
at once without more argument,
(putting his hand to his sword)
you'll repent it.

6. ARIA

MASETTO
(to Don Giovanni)
Oh yes, I understand, sir!
I bow my head and go.
Since you will it so,
I'll hold my tongue.
You're a gentleman,
of that I'm in no doubt, indeed:
that's clear from the gracious favour
you bestow on me.
(to Zerlina, aside)
Wanton hussy!
you've undone me!
*(to Leporello, who is trying to
lead him away)*
Yes, I'm coming!
(to Zerlina)
Stay then!

42

E una cosa molto onesta;	There's a fine thing!
faccia il nostro cavaliere	Let my lord make
cavaliera ancora te.	a lady of you!

*(Masetto parte con Leporello
ed i Contadini)*

*(exit Masetto with Leporello and
the villagers)*

SCENA NONA

SCENE 9

Don Giovanni e Zerlina

Don Giovanni and Zerlina

RECITATIVO

RECITATIVE

GIOVANNI
Alfin siam liberati,
Zerlinetta gentil, da quel scioccone
Che ne dite, mio ben, so far pulito?

GIOVANNI
At last, sweet Zerlina,
we are free of that booby.
Wasn't it neatly done?

ZERLINA
Signore, è mio marito . . .

ZERLINA
My lord, he's to be my husband . . .

GIOVANNI
Chi? colui?
Vi par che un onest'uomo,
un nobil cavalier, com'io mi vanto,
possa soffrir che quel visetto d'oro,
quel viso inzuccherato
da un bifolcaccio vil sia strapazzato?

GIOVANNI
What, he?
Do you think a man of honour,
a nobleman, as I am proud to be,
could allow so sweet and lovely a face
to be wasted
on an oafish bumpkin?

ZERLINA
Ma, signore, io gli diedi
parola di sposarlo.

ZERLINA
But, my lord,
I have promised to marry him.

GIOVANNI
Tal parola
non vale un zero. Voi non siete fatta
per essere paesana; un'altra sorte
vi procuran quegli occhi bricconcelli,
que' labretti si belli,
quelle ditucce candide e odorose:
parmi toccar giuncata e fiutar rose.

GIOVANNI
Such a promise
is worth nothing. You were not created
to be a peasant: another fate
awaits those roguish eyes,
those lovely lips,
those slender fingers,
white as curds and fragrant as roses.

ZERLINA
Ah! . . . non vorrei . . .

ZERLINA
I'm afraid . . .

GIOVANNI
Che non vorresti?

GIOVANNI
Afraid of what?

ZERLINA
Alfine ingannata restar. Io so che
raro colle donne voi altri cavalieri
siete onesti e sinceri.

GIOVANNI
E un'impostura
della gente plebea. La nobiltà
ha dipinta negli occhi l'onestà.
Orsu, non perdiam tempo;
in questo istante io ti voglio sposar.

ZERLINA
Voi!

GIOVANNI
Certo, io.
Quel casinetto è mio: soli saremo,
e là, gioiello mio, ci sposeremo.

7. DUETTINO

GIOVANNI
Là ci darem la mano,
là mi dirai di sì.
Vedi, non è lontano:
partiam, ben mio, da qui.

ZERLINA
(tra sé)
Vorrei, e non vorrei . . .
Mi trema un poco il cor . . .
Felice, è ver, sarei:
ma può burlarmi ancor.

GIOVANNI
Vieni, mio bel diletto!

ZERLINA
(tra sé)
Mi fa pietà Masetto!

GIOVANNI
Io cangerò tua sorte.

ZERLINA
Presto . . . non son più forte.

ZERLINA E GIOVANNI
Andiam, andiam, mio bene,
a ristorar le pene

ZERLINA
Of being forsaken afterwards.
I know how seldom you fine gentlemen
are open and honest with us girls.

GIOVANNI
That's a slander of low minds.
A nobleman's honour
is written in his face.
Come, let's not waste time:
this very moment I'll make you my bride.

ZERLINA
You will?

GIOVANNI
Of course I will.
That villa is mine: we'll be alone,
and there, my jewel, we'll be united.

7. DUETTINO

GIOVANNI
There we'll take hands,
and you will whisper "Yes".
See, it's close by:
let's leave this place, my dear.

ZERLINA
(aside)
I'd like to, but I dare not . . .
My heart will not be still . . .
I know I would be happy;
but he may yet deceive me.

GIOVANNI
Come, my dear treasure!

ZERLINA
(aside)
I'm sorry for Masetto.

GIOVANNI
I'll change your fate.

ZERLINA
Quick then . . . I can resist no longer.

BOTH
Then come, oh come, my dearest,
and ease the ache

44

d'un innocente amor!	of a chaste love!
(si incamminano abbracciati *verso il casino)*	*(they go towards the house,* *arm in arm)*

SCENA DECIMA

SCENE 10

Donna Elvira e detti

Donna Elvira and the above

RECITATIVO

RECITATIVE

ELVIRA
(che ferma con atti disperatissimi
Don Giovanni)
Férmati, scellerato! Il ciel mi fece
udir le tue perfidie. Io sono a tempo
di salvar questa misera innocente
dal tuo barbaro artiglio.

ELVIRA
(desperately intercepting
Don Giovanni)
Stay, villain! Heaven has made me
witness of your perfidy. I am in time
to save this poor innocent
from your heartless clutches.

ZERLINA
Meschina! cosa sento!

ZERLINA
Alas! what do I hear?

GIOVANNI
(tra sé)
Amor, consiglio.
(piano a Donna Elvira)
Idol mio, non vedete
ch'io voglio divertirmi?

GIOVANNI
(aside)
Love, inspire me!
(softly to Donna Elvira)
Don't you see, my angel,
that I'm just amusing myself?

ELVIRA
(ad alta voce)
Divertirti,
è vero? divertirti . . . Io so, crudele,
come tu ti diverti.

ELVIRA
(aloud)
Amusing yourself indeed!
Amusing yourself . . . I know, cruel man,
how you amuse yourself.

ZERLINA
Ma, signor cavaliere,
è ver quel ch'ella dice?

ZERLINA
But my lord,
is it true what she's saying?

GIOVANNI
(piano a Zerlina)
La povera infelice
è di me innamorata,
e per pietà deggio fingere amore,
ch'io son, per mia disgrazia,
uom di buon cuore.

GIOVANNI
(softly to Zerlina)
The poor unhappy lady
is infatuated with me,
and in pity I must pretend to love her too:
I am, I'm afraid,
so tender-hearted.

8. ARIA

ELVIRA
Ah, fuggi il traditor,
non lo lasciar più dir:
il labbro è mentitor,
fallace il ciglio.
Da'miei tormenti impara
a credere a quel cor,
e nasca il tuo timor
dal mio periglio.

(parte conducendo via Zerlina)

SCENA UNDICESIMA

*Don Giovanni, poi Don Ottavio
e Donna Anna vestita a lutto*

RECITATIVO

GIOVANNI
Mi par ch'oggi il demonio si diverta
d'opporsi a' miei piacevoli progressi;
vanno mal tutti quanti.

OTTAVIO
(a Donna Anna)
Ah! ch'ora, idolo mio,
son vani i pianti;
di vendetta si parli . . .
Ah, Don Giovanni!

GIOVANNI
(tra sé)
Mancava questo inver!

ANNA
Amico, a tempo
vi ritroviam: avete core, avete
anima generosa?

GIOVANNI
(tra sé)
Sta a vedere che il diavolo
le ha detto qualche cosa.
(forte)
Che domanda! perché?

8. ARIA

ELVIRA
Ah, flee the traitor,
and let him cozen you no more:
deceit is on his lips
and falsehood in his eyes.
From my sufferings learn
what it means to trust him;
and be warned in time
by my plight.

(exit, leading Zerlina away)

SCENE XI

*Don Giovanni, then Don Ottavio
and Donna Anna in mourning*

RECITATIVE

GIOVANNI
It seems as if the devil's taking sport
today in thwarting all my pleasant plans:
all are going astray.

OTTAVIO
(to Donna Anna)
Ah, dearest,
tears serve no purpose now:
let us speak instead of vengeance . . .
Oh, Don Giovanni

GIOVANNI
(aside)
This is all it needed!

ANNA
My friend, we meet most opportunely.
Have you courage,
have you a generous spirit?

GIOVANNI
(aside)
I'm sure the devil
has put her on the track.
(aloud)
Strange questions! Why?

46

OTTAVIO	OTTAVIO
Bisogno abbiamo della	We have sore need of
vostra amicizia.	your friendship.
GIOVANNI	GIOVANNI
(tra sé)	*(aside)*
Mi torna il fiato in corpo.	I breathe again more freely.
(forte)	*(aloud)*
Comandate ...	Yours to command ...
I congiunti, i parenti, questa man,	my friends and relations,
questo ferro, i beni, il sangue	this hand, this sword, my possessions,
spenderò per servirvi.	my blood I'll give to serve you.
Ma voi, bella Donna Anna,	But, dear Donna Anna,
perché così piangete?	why do you weep so?
Il crudele chi fu che osò la calma	What viper has dared to trouble
turbar del viver vostro?	the calm of your existence?

SCENA DODICESIMA — SCENE 12

Donna Elvira e detti — *Donna Elvira and the above*

ELVIRA	ELVIRA
(a Don Giovanni)	*(to Don Giovanni)*
Ah! ti ritrovo ancor,	Ah! I find you again,
perfido mostro!	perfidious monster!

9. QUARTETTO — 9. QUARTET

ELVIRA	ELVIRA
(a Donna Anna)	*(to Donna Anna)*
Non ti fidar, o misera,	Unhappy woman, do not trust
di quel ribaldo cor;	that false man:
me già tradì quel barbaro,	already he's betrayed me,
te vuol tradire ancor.	he'll do the same to you.
ANNA ED OTTAVIO	ANNA AND OTTAVIO
(tra loro)	*(aside)*
Cieli, che aspetto nobile!	How noble is her bearing!
Che dolce maestà!	What dignity and sweetness!
Il suo pallor, le lagrime,	Her pallor and her tears
m'empiono di pietà.	fill me with pity.
GIOVANNI	GIOVANNI
(a parte; Donna Elvira ascolta)	*(aside: Donna Elvira listens)*
La povera ragazza	Dear friends, this poor girl's
è pazza, amici miei;	lost her reason;
lasciatemi con lei,	leave her with me,
forse si calmerà.	then perhaps she'll calm herself.

ELVIRA
(a Donna Anna e Don Ottavio)
Ah! non credete al perfido;
restate ancor, restate . . .

ELVIRA
(to Donna Anna and Don Ottavio)
Ah, do not believe his falsehoods:
stay, I beg you, stay . . .

GIOVANNI
È pazza, non badate . . .

GIOVANNI
She's crazy: take no notice.

ANNA ED OTTAVIO
A chi si crederà?
(tra loro)
Certo moto d'ignoto tormento
dentro l'alma girare mi sento,
che mi dice per quella infelice
cento cose che intender non sa.

ANNA AND OTTAVIO
Which am I to believe?
(aside)
I feel some strange suspicion
stirring in my breast
which tells me, by this unhappy girl,
a host of things I barely understand.

ELVIRA
(tra sé)
Sdegno, rabbia, dispetto, spavento
dentro l'alma girare mi sento,
che mi dice di quel traditore
cento cose che intender non sa.

ELVIRA
(aside)
Scorn, anger, spite and dread
are raging in my bosom,
telling me of this traitor
a host of things I barely understand.

GIOVANNI
(tra sé)
Certo moto d'ignoto spavento
dentro l'alma girare mi sento,
che mi dice per quella infelice
cento cose che intender non sa.

GIOVANNI
(aside)
I feel some strange suspicion
stirring in my breast
which tells me, by this unhappy girl,
a host of things I barely understand.

OTTAVIO
(a Donna Anna) .
Io di qua non vado via
se non scopro quest' affar.

OTTAVIO
(to Donna Anna)
I'll not go from here
until I've solved this matter.

ANNA
(a Don Ottavio)
Non ha l'aria di pazzia
il suo tratto, il suo parlar.

ANNA
(to Don Ottavio)
Neither in manner nor in speech
does she seem mad.

GIOVANNI
(tra sé)
Se men vado, si potria
qualche cosa sospettar.

GIOVANNI
(aside)
If I leave them,
it may look suspicious.

ELVIRA
(a Donna Anna e Don Ottavio)
Da quel ceffo si dovria
la ner'alma giudicar.

ELVIRA
(to Donna Anna and Don Ottavio)
You can see his black villainy
in his face.

OTTAVIO
(a Don Giovanni)
Dunque quella?. . .

GIOVANNI
È pazzerella.

ANNA
(a Donna Elvira)
Dunque quegli? . . .

ELVIRA
È un traditore.

GIOVANNI
Infelice!

ELVIRA
Mentitore!

ANNA ED OTTAVIO
Incomincio a dubitar.

(Passano dei contadini)

GIOVANNI
(piano a Donna Elvira)
Zitto, zitto, ché la gente
si raduna a noi d'intorno.
Siate un poco più prudente:
vi farete criticar.

ELVIRA
(forte, a Don Giovanni)
Non sperarlo, o scellerato:
ho perduto la prudenza.
Le tue colpe ed il mio stato
voglio a tutti palesar.

ANNA ED OTTAVIO
(a parte, guardando Don Giovanni)
Quegli accenti si sommessi,
quel cangiarsi di colore,
sono indizi troppo espressi
che mi fan determinar.

(Donna Elvira parte)

OTTAVIO
(to Don Giovanni)
So you say she's . . . ?

GIOVANNI
She's demented.

ANNA
(to Donna Elvira)
And you say he's . . .?

ELVIRA
He's a traitor.

GIOVANNI
Poor creature!

ELVIRA
He's a liar!

ANNA AND OTTAVIO
I begin to have doubts.

(Villagers go by)

GIOVANNI
(softly to Donna Elvira)
Do be quiet,
or you'll bring a crowd about us:
be more discreet,
or you'll create a scandal.

ELVIRA
(loudly to Don Giovanni)
Do not think to silence me, you villain:
it is too late for discretion.
I'll proclaim your baseness
and my plight from the rooftops.

ANNA AND OTTAVIO
(aside, watching Don Giovanni)
These low whisperings
and his change of colour
are signs too revealing
that make things clear to me.

(exit Donna Elvira)

RECITATIVO

GIOVANNI
Povera sventurata! i passi suoi
voglio seguir, non voglio
che faccia un precipizio:
perdonate, bellissima Donna Anna:
se servirvi poss'io,
in mia casa v'aspetto;
amici, addio!

(parte frettoloso)

SCENA TREDICESIMA

Donna Anna e Don Ottavio

10. RECITATIVO ED ARIA

ANNA
Don Ottavio . . . son morta!

OTTAVIO
Cos'è stato?

ANNA
Per pietà, soccorretemi.

OTTAVIO
Mio bene, fate coraggio.

ANNA
Oh Dei! quegli è il carnefice
del padre mio . . .

OTTAVIO
Che dite?

ANNA
Non dubitate più. Gli ultimi accenti,
che l'empio proferi, tutta la voce
richiamâr nel cor mio di quell'indegno
che nel mio appartamento . . .

OTTAVIO
Oh ciel! possibile
che sotto il sacro manto
d'amicizia . . .
Ma come fu, narratemi
lo strano avvenimento.

RECITATIVE

GIOVANNI
Poor afflicted creature! I will follow
her steps for fear
she commit some folly.
Excuse me, fair Donna Anna;
if I can be of service,
you have but to call on me.
Farewell, friends!

(exit hurriedly)

SCENE 13

Donna Anna and Don Ottavio

10. RECITATIVE AND ARIA

ANNA
Don Ottavio . . . I'm fainting!

OTTAVIO
What has happened?

ANNA
In pity's name, support me.

OTTAVIO
My dearest, take courage.

ANNA
O Heaven! that is the man
who slew my father . . .

OTTAVIO
What say you?

ANNA
I can no longer doubt it.
The last words he uttered, his whole voice,
recall to me the intruder
who came into my chamber . . .

OTTAVIO
Great Heavens! is it possible
that beneath the sacred cloak
of friendship . . . ?
But tell me more exactly
of this dire adventure.

50

ANNA
Era già alquanto
avanzata la notte,
quando nelle mie stanze, ove soletta
mi trovai per sventura, entrar io vidi
in un mantello avvolto
un uom che al primo istante
avea preso per voi;
ma riconobbi poi
che un inganno era il mio . . .

OTTAVIO
(con affanno)
Stelle! seguite.

ANNA
Tacito a me s'appressa,
e mi vuol abbracciar; sciogliermi
cerco, ei più mi stringe; io grido:
non vien alcun: con una mano cerca
d'impedire la voce,
e coll'altra m'afferra
stretta cosi, che già mi
credo vinta.

OTTAVIO
Perfido! alfin?

ANNA
Alfine il duol, l'orrore
dell'infame attentato
accrebber si la lena mia che a forza
di svincolarmi, torcermi e piegarmi,
da lui mi sciolsi.

OTTAVIO
Ahimè! respiro.

ANNA
Allora rinforzo i stridi miei,
chiamo soccorso, fugge il fellon;
arditamente il seguo fin nella
strada per fermarlo, e sono
assalitrice ed assalita: il padre
v'accorre, vuol conoscerlo,
e l'indegno che del povero
vecchio era più forte, compie
il misfatto suo col dargli morte.

ANNA
It was already somewhat late at night,
and I was all alone, as misfortune
would have it, in my room,
when a man came in
with his cloak about him,
who for the moment
I thought was you;
but I soon found
how great was my mistake . . .

OTTAVIO
(anxiously)
Horror! go on.

ANNA
Silently he drew near me
and made to embrace me:
I tried to free myself,
he seized me closer;
I screamed for help, but no one came;
with one hand he sought to stifle my cries,
with the other he held me so tight
that I feared all was lost.

OTTAVIO
Horrible! and then?

ANNA
At last my shame, my horror
at this vile attack,
lent me such strength
that by dint of struggling, writhing
and twisting I broke loose from him.

OTTAVIO
Thank God! I breathe again.

ANNA
Then I redoubled my cries
and called for help; he took to flight:
boldly I pursued him into the street
to stop him — now I was assailing
the assailant; my father appeared
and challenged him, but the miscreant,
who was much stronger than my poor
old father, rounded off his crime
by killing him.

51

(ARIA)

ANNA
Or sai chi l'onore
rapire a me volse:
chi fu il traditore,
che il padre mi tolse:
vendetta ti chiedo,
la chiede il tuo cor.
Rammenta la piaga
del misero seno:
rimira di sangue
coperto il terreno,
se l'ira in te langue
d'un giusto furor.

(parte)

SCENA QUATTORDICESIMA

Ottavio solo

RECITATIVO

OTTAVIO
Come mai creder deggio
di sì nero delitto
capace un cavaliero!
Ah, di scoprire il vero ogni mezzo
si cerchi. Io sento in petto
e di sposo e d'amico
il dover che mi parla:
disingannarla voglio o vendicarla.

10a. ARIA

OTTAVIO
Dalla sua pace la mia dipende,
quel che a lei piace vita mi rende,
quel che le incresce morte mi dà.
S'ella sospira, sospiro anch'io,
è mia quell'ira, quel pianto e mio
e non ho bene s'ella non l'ha.

(parte)

SCENA QUINDICESIMA

Leporello, poi Don Giovanni

(ARIA)

ANNA
Now you know who sought
to steal my honour,
who was my betrayer
and my father's murderer:
I ask of you vengeance,
your heart asks it too.
Remember the wound
gaping in his breast,
recall the earth
covered with his blood,
if ever the wrath of a just fury
should weaken in you.

(exit)

SCENE 14

Don Ottavio alone

RECITATIVE

OTTAVIO
I can scarcely believe
a nobleman capable
of so atrocious a crime!
I will pursue every means
to discover the truth.
In my heart I feel the call of duty,
both as her betrothed and his friend,
either to undeceive her or avenge her.

10a ARIA

OTTAVIO
On her peace of mind depends mine too:
what pleases her gives life to me,
what grieves her wounds me to the heart.
If she sighs, I sigh with her;
her anger and her sorrow are mine,
and joy I cannot know unless she share it.

(exit)

SCENE 15

Leporello, then Don Giovanni

52

RECITATIVO

LEPORELLO
Io deggio, ad ogni patto,
per sempre abbandonar questo
bel matto . . . Eccolo qua: guardate
con qual indifferenza se ne viene!

GIOVANNI
Oh Leporello mio! va tutto bene?

LEPORELLO
Don Giovannino mio! va tutto male.

GIOVANNI
Come va tutto male?

LEPORELLO
Vado a casa,
come voi m'ordinaste,
con tutta quella gente.

GIOVANNI
Bravo!

LEPORELLO
A forza
di chiacchiere, di vezzi e di bugie,
ch'ho imparato si bene a star con
voi, cerco d'intrattenerli.

GIOVANNI
Bravo!

LEPORELLO
Dico
mille cose a Masetto per placarlo,
per trargli dal pensier la gelosia.

GIOVANNI
Bravo, in coscienza mia!

LEPORELLO
Faccio che bevano
e gli uomini e le donne;
son già mezzo ubbriachi,
altri canta, altri scherza,
altri seguita a ber . . .
In sul più bello,
chi credete che capiti?

RECITATIVE

LEPORELLO
I must at all costs have done
for good with this fine madman!
Here he comes: look at him,
how coolly he's behaving!

GIOVANNI
My worthy Leporello! is all going well?

LEPORELLO
Worthy Don Giovanni, all's going badly.

GIOVANNI
Why going badly?

LEPORELLO
I went home,
as you ordered me,
with all those people.

GIOVANNI
Bravo!

LEPORELLO
With chattering,
flattery and humbug,
which I've picked up so well
in your service, I tried to entertain them.

GIOVANNI
Bravo!

LEPORELLO
I said all I could
to placate Masetto
and turn his thoughts from jealousy . . .

GIOVANNI
Well done, upon my word!

LEPORELLO
I got them drinking,
both the men and the women,
until they were half tipsy:
some were singing, some making merry,
some drinking solidly . . .
All was going well,
when who burst in upon us?.

GIOVANNI
Zerlina!

LEPORELLO
Bravo! e con lei chi venne?

GIOVANNI
Donna Elvira!

LEPORELLO
Bravo! e disse di voi?

GIOVANNI
Tutto quel mal
che in bocca le venia.

LEPORELLO
Bravo, in coscienza mia!

GIOVANNI
E tu cosa facesti?

LEPORELLO
Tacqui.

GIOVANNI
Ed ella?

LEPORELLO
Seguì a gridar.

GIOVANNI
E tu?

LEPORELLO
Quando mi parve
che già fosse sfogata, dolcemente
fuor dell'orto la trassi, e con
bell'arte, chiusa la porta a chiave;
io di là mi cavai,
e sulla via soletta la lasciai.

GIOVANNI
Bravo! bravo, arcibravo!
L'affar non può andar meglio.
Incominciasti, io saprò terminar;
troppo mi premono queste
contadinotte: le voglio divertir
finché vien notte.

GIOVANNI
Zerlina.

LEPORELLO
Bravo! and who was with her?

GIOVANNI
Donna Elvira.

LEPORELLO
Bravo! and she called you?

GIOVANNI
Every name
that she could think of.

LEPORELLO
Well done, upon my word!

GIOVANNI
And what did you do then?

LEPORELLO
Kept quiet.

GIOVANNI
And she?

LEPORELLO
She went on raving.

GIOVANNI
And you?

LEPORELLO
When it seemed
that she was tiring,
I led her gently out of the garden, and
very neatly locked the gate behind her.
then made myself scarce
and left her alone on the street.

GIOVANNI
Leporello, you're a genius!
You couldn't have done better.
Now what you've started I
can finish. These country wenches
attract me: I'll amuse them
until nightfall.

11. ARIA

GIOVANNI
Fin ch'han dal vino
calda la testa,
una gran festa
fa preparar.
Se trovi in piazza
qualche ragazza,
teco ancor quella
cerca menar.
Senza alcun ordine
la danza sia:
chi il minuetto,
chi la follia,
chi l'alemanna
farai ballar.
Ed io frattanto
dall'altro canto
con questa e quella
vo' amoreggiar.
Ah! la mia lista
doman mattina
d'una decina
devi aumentar.

(partono)

SCENA SEDICESIMA

*Giardino con due porte chiuse a
chiave per di fuori. Due nicchie.
Zerlina, Masetto e Contadini.*

RECITATIVO

ZERLINA
Masetto . . . senti un po' . . .
Masetto, dico . . .

MASETTO
Non mi toccar.

ZERLINA
Perché?

MASETTO
Perche mi chiedi?
Perfida! il tatto sopportar dovrei
d'una mano infedele?

11. ARIA

GIOVANNI
Now prepare
a great feast
until the wine
makes all heads reel:
any girls you may find
in the square,
bring them
along too.
Let the dancing be wild
and abandoned:
give them here
a minuet,
here a folia,
there an allemande.
Meantime I will have
my own fun,
making love
to one or other.
Ah! by tomorrow evening
my list
should be a dozen
to the good.

(exeunt)

SCENE 16

*A garden with two doors locked
from outside. Two alcoves.
Zerlina, Masetto and villagers.*

RECITATIVE

ZERLINA
Masetto, just listen . . .
Masetto, please . . .

MASETTO
Leave me alone.

ZERLINA
But why?

MASETTO
Why? You can ask that?
Hussy! I'll not have that faithless hand
so much as touch me.

ZERLINA
Ah! no: taci, crudele!
Io non merto da te
tal trattamento.

MASETTO
Come! ed hai l'ardimento di scusarti?
Star sola con un uom!
Abbandonarmi il di delle mie nozze!
Porre in fronte a un villano d'onore
questa marca d'infamia!
Ah! se non fosse,
se non fosse lo scandalo, vorrei . . .

ZERLINA
Ma se colpa io non ho: ma se da lui
ingannata rimasi; e poi, che temi?
Tranquillati, mia vita,
non mi toccò la punta delle dita.
Non me lo credi? Ingrato!
Vien qui, sfogati, ammazzami,
fa tutto di me quel che ti piace,
ma poi, Masetto mio,
ma poi fa pace.

12. ARIA

ZERLINA
Batti, batti, o bel Masetto,
la tua povera Zerlina:
starò qui come agnellina
le tue botte ad aspettar.
Lascerò straziarmi il crine,
lascerò cavarmi gli occhi;
e le care tue manine
lieta poi saprò baciar.
Ah! lo vedo, non hai core:
pace, pace, o vita mia!
In contento ed allegria
notte e di vogliam passar.

(parte)

SCENA DICIASSETTESIMA

*Masetto, poi Don Giovanni di
dentro e di nuovo Zerlina*

ZERLINA
Oh please don't be so cruel!
I don't deserve
such unkindness from you.

MASETTO
What! You have the face to make excuses'
To leave me and go off with another man
on our wedding day itself!
To bring shame on one who's
poor but honest!
Oh, if it weren't for the scandal
there'd be, I'd . . .

ZERLINA
But I've done nothing wrong: if he
dazzled me for the moment, there's no
need to fear now. Don't be so angry,
dearest: he didn't lay a finger on me.
Won't you believe me? Sulky!
Well then, come and beat me black and
blue, do what you like with me —
and then, darling Masetto,
let's make it up again.

12. ARIA

ZERLINA
Beat me, dear Masetto,
beat your poor Zerlina.
I'll stand here as meek as a lamb
and bear the blows you lay on me.
You can tear my hair out,
put out my eyes,
yet gladly I'll kiss
your dear hands.
Ah! I see you've no mind to:
let's make peace, dearest love!
In happiness and joy
let's pass our days and nights.

(exit)

SCENE 17

*Masetto, then Don Giovanni within
and Zerlina again*

56

RECITATIVO	RECITATIVE

MASETTO
Guarda un po' come seppe
questa strega sedurmi! Siamo pure
i deboli di testa!

MASETTO
You see how this little witch
gets round me! We men
are weak-minded.

GIOVANNI
(di dentro)
Sia preparato tutto
a una gran festa.

GIOVANNI
(from within)
See that everything is prepared
for a splendid entertainment.

ZERLINA
(rientrando)
Ah! Masetto, Masetto, udii la
voce del monsù cavaliero!

ZERLINA
(returning)
Masetto, listen!
That's his lordship's voice!

MASETTO
Ebben, che c'è?

MASETTO
Well, what of it?

ZERLINA
Verrà . . .

ZERLINA
He's coming . . .

MASETTO
Lascia che venga.

MASETTO
Let him come then.

ZERLINA
Ah! se vi fosse
un buco da fuggir!

ZERLINA
If there were but
some hole to hide in!

MASETTO
Di cosa temi? Perché diventi
pallida? . . . Ah! capisco:
capisco, bricconcella, hai timor
ch'io comprenda com'è tra voi
passata la faccenda.

MASETTO
What are you afraid of?
Why do you turn pale? . . .
Ah! I see!
Hussy! you're afraid I shall find out
what went on between you.

13. FINALE

13. FINALE

MASETTO
Presto, presto . . . pria ch'ei venga,
por mi vo' da qualche lato . . .
C'è una nicchia . . . qui celato
cheto, cheto mi vo' star.

MASETTO
Then quickly, before he comes,
I'll stand aside somewhere.
Here's an alcove . . .
I'll slip in here and hide.

ZERLINA
Senti, senti . . . dove vai?
Non t'asconder, o Masetto.
Si ti trova, poveretto!
tu non sai quel che può far.

ZERLINA
Wait a moment! Where are you off to?
Don't hide yourself, Masetto,
for if he finds you,
you don't know what he may do.

MASETTO
Faccia, dica quel che vuole.

ZERLINA
(sotto voce)
Ah, non giovan le parole . . .

MASETTO
Parla forte, e qui ti arresta.

ZERLINA
Che capriccio hai nella testa!

MASETTO
(tra sé)
Capirò se m'è fedele,
e in qual modo ando l'affar.

(entra nella nicchia)

ZERLINA
(tra sé)
Quell'ingrato, quel crudele
oggi vuol precipitar.

SCENA DICIOTESIMA

*Don Giovanni, Contadini e Servi,
Zerlina e Masetto nascosto*

GIOVANNI
Su, svegliatevi; da bravi!
Su, coraggio, o buona gente;
vogliam stare allegramente,
vogliam ridere e scherzar.
(ai servi)
Alla stanza della danza
conducete tutti quanti
ed a tutti in abbondanza
gran rinfreschi fate dar.

CORO
(partendo co' servi)
Su, svegliatevi; . . .

SCENA DICIANNOVESIMA

*Don Giovanni, Zerlina e Masetto
nascosto*

MASETTO
He can do or say what he likes.

ZERLINA
(sotto voce)
All my words are wasted on him . . .

MASETTO
Speak up . . . and stay here.

ZERLINA
He's so pig-headed!

MASETTO
(aside)
I must know if she is faithful,
and what's the truth of this affair.

(goes into an alcove)

ZERLINA
(aside)
His unkindness and suspicion
will end us up in trouble.

SCENE 18

*Don Giovanni, villagers and servants,
Zerlina, and Masetto concealed*

GIOVANNI
Come, good people, rouse yourselves!
Be of good cheer!
We'll have gaiety
and mirth and sport.
(to the servants)
Lead all the guests
into the rooms for dancing,
and let there be food and drink
for all in plenty.

CHORUS
(going with the servants)
Come, good people . . .

SCENE 19

*Don Giovanni, Zerlina, and Masetto
concealed*

ZERLINA
Tra quest'arbori celata
si può dar che non mi veda.
(vuol nascondersi)

ZERLINA
If I hide among these trees
perhaps he will not see me.
(she tries to hide)

GIOVANNI
Zerlinetta mia garbata,
ti ho già vista, non scappar.
(la prende)

GIOVANNI
Sweet Zerlina, I can see you:
don't run away!
(he detains her)

ZERLINA
Ah! lasciatemi andar via . . .

ZERLINA
Oh please let me go.

GIOVANNI
No, no, resta, gioia mia!

GIOVANNI
No, no, stay here, my fairest!

ZERLINA
Se pietade avete in core!

ZERLINA
If you have any pity in your heart!

GIOVANNI
Sì, bien mio! son tutto amore.
Vieni un poco in questo loco,
fortunata io ti vo' far.

GIOVANNI
Ah, my dear, my heart is full of love.
Come a moment into this arbour
and I'll make you happy.

ZERLINA
(tra sé)
Ah! se il vede il sposo mio.
so ben io quel che può far.

ZERLINA
(aside)
Ah! if Masetto sees me,
I'm terrified what he'll do.

GIOVANNI
*(nell'aprire la nicchia scopre
Masetto)*
Masetto!

GIOVANNI
*(going into the alcove, discovers
Masetto)*
Masetto!

MASETTO
Sì, Masetto.

MASETTO
Yes, Masetto!

GIOVANNI
(un po' confuso)
E chiuso là, perché?
(riprende ardire)
La bella tua Zerlina non può,
la poverina, più star senza di te.

GIOVANNI
(somewhat confused)
And why in hiding there?
(recovering his boldness)
Your poor little Zerlina
needs you with her.

MASETTO
(ironico)
Capisco, sì, signore..

MASETTO
(ironically)
Yes indeed, sir.

GIOVANNI
Adesso fate core.
(s'ode un'orchestra in lontananza)

GIOVANNI
Then come and make merry.
(an orchestra is heard in the distance)

I suonatori udite:
venite omai con me.

Hark to the music!
Come along with me.

MASETTO E ZERLINA
Sì, sì, facciamo core,
ed a ballar cogli altri
andiamo tutti tre.

MASETTO AND ZERLINA
Yes, let's make merry,
and all three
join the dancing.

(partono)

(exeunt)

SCENA VENTESIMA

SCENE 20

*Si va facendo notte. Don Ottavio,
Donna Anna e Donna Elvira
in maschera; poi Leporello e
Don Giovanni alla finestra*

*It is getting dark. Don Ottavio
Donna Anna and Donna Elvira
masked; then Leporello and
Don Giovanni at the window*

ELVIRA
Bisogna aver coraggio,
o cari amici miei,
e i suoi misfatti rei
scoprir potremo allor.

ELVIRA
Now steel ourselves,
dear friends, to courage,
and we'll expose
his wicked crimes.

OTTAVIO
L'amica dice bene;
coraggio aver conviene.
(a Donna Anna)
Discaccia, o vita mia,
l'affanno ed il timor.

OTTAVIO
Our friend is right:
we must have courage.
(to Donna Anna)
No time now, my love,
for distress or fear.

ANNA
Il passo è periglioso,
può nascer qualche imbroglio;
temo pel caro sposo
(a Donna Elvira)
e per voi temo ancor.

ANNA
The step we take is dangerous,
and none can guess its outcome.
I fear for you, dear husband,
(to Donna Elvira)
and for our friend here too.

LEPORELLO
(aprendo la finestra)
Signor, guardate un poco
che maschere galanti!

LEPORELLO
(opening the window)
Sir, come and see
these charming maskers!

GIOVANNI
(alla finestra)
Falle passare avanti,
di' che ci fanno onor.

GIOVANNI
(at the window)
Ask them to come in
and honour our revels.

ANNA, ELVIRE ED OTTAVIO
(tra loro)
Al volto ed alla voce

ANNA, ELVIRA AND OTTAVIO
(aside)
That voice and manner

si scopre il traditor.

LEPORELLO
Zì, zì, signore maschere . . .

ANNA ED ELVIRA
(a Don Ottavio)
Via, rispondete.

LEPORELLO
Zì, zì . . .

OTTAVIO
Cosa chiedete?

LEPORELLO
Al ballo, se vi piace,
v'invita il mio signor.

OTTAVIO
Grazie di tanto onore.
Andiam, compagne belle.

LEPORELLO
(tra sé)
L'amico anche su quelle
prova farà d'amor.
(entra e chiude la finestra)

ANNA ED OTTAVIO
Protegga il giusto cielo
lo zelo del mio cor.

ELVIRA
Vendichi il giusto cielo
il mio tradito amor.

(entrano)

SCENA VENTUNESIMA

*Sala nella casa di Don Giovanni,
illuminata e preparata per una
gran festa da ballo.
Don Giovanni, Leporello, Zerlina,
Masetto, Contadini e Contadine,
servitori con rinfreschi; poi
Don Ottavio, Donna Anna e Donna
Elvira in maschera. Don Giovanni
fa seder le ragazze e Leporello i*

reveal him as the traitor.

LEPORELLO
Pst! pst! you fair maskers!

ANNA AND ELVIRA
(to Don Ottavio)
Go on, reply to him.

LEPORELLO
Pst! pst!

OTTAVIO
What is it, sir?

LEPORELLO
My master sends his compliments
and invites you to the ball.

OTTAVIO
Tell him we'd be honoured.
Come, my dear companions.

LEPORELLO
(aside)
My lord has two more
for his bag.
(goes in and shuts the window)

ANNA AND OTTAVIO
May a just Heaven
protect my heart's purpose.

ELVIRA
May a just Heaven
avenge my outraged love.

(they go in)

SCENE 21

*Hall in Don Giovanni's house,
lit up and decorated for a
festive ball.
Don Giovanni, Leporello, Zerlina,
Masetto, villagers, stage bands,
servants with refreshments; then
Don Ottavio, Donna Anna and
Donna Elvira masked. Don Giovanni
is handing some girls to seats,*

61

ragazzi che saranno in atto d'aver finito un ballo.

GIOVANNI
Riposate, vezzose ragazze.

LEPORELLO
Rinfrescatevi, bei giovinotti.

GIOVANNI E LEPORELLO
Tornerete a far presto le pazze,
tornerete a scherzar e ballar.

GIOVANNI
Eh! caffè.

LEPORELLO
Cioccolata.

MASETTO
(piano a Zerlina)
Ah! Zerlina, giudizio!

GIOVANNI
Sorbetti.

LEPORELLO
Confetti.

ZERLINA E MASETTO
(a parte)
Troppo dolce comincia la scena.
In amaro potria terminar.

(Vengono portati e distribuiti i rinfreschi)

GIOVANNI
(accarezzando Zerlina)
Sei pur vaga, brillante Zerlina!

ZERLINA
Sua bontà.

MASETTO
(tra sé, fremendo)
La briccona fa festa.

LEPORELLO
(imitando il padrone)
Sei pur cara, Giannotta, Sandrina!

Leporello the youths: a dance has just finished.

GIOVANNI
Pretty maidens, rest for a moment.

LEPORELLO
Do take a drink, gentlemen.

GIOVANNI AND LEPORELLO
Then return to the revels,
to mirth and to dancing once more.

GIOVANNI
Ho! some coffee!

LEPORELLO
Chocolate!

MASETTO
(softly to Zerlina)
Now, Zerlina, be careful!

GIOVANNI
Ices!

LEPORELLO
Sweetmeats!

ZERLINA AND MASETTO
(aside)
Everything's going too gaily:
the sweet may yet turn to sour.

(Refreshments are brought in and handed round)

GIOVANNI
(caressing Zerlina)
You look lovely, my little Zerlina!

ZERLINA
Oh, my lord!

MASETTO
(aside, fuming)
The minx is flirting again.

LEPORELLO
(imitating his master)
You look lovely, Giannotta, Sandrina!

MASETTO
(guardando Don Giovanni, tra sé)
Tocca pur, che ti cada la testa.

MASETTO
(aside, watching Don Giovanni)
Just touch her, and I'll have your head!

ZERLINA
(tra sé)
Quel Masetto mi par stralunato.
Brutto, brutto si fa quest'affar.

ZERLINA
(aside)
Poor Masetto is losing his temper:
I'm afraid there is trouble ahead.

GIOVANNI E LEPORELLO
(tra sé)
Quel Masetto mi par stralunato.
Qui bisogna cervello adoprar.

GIOVANNI AND LEPORELLO
(aside)
That Masetto is losing his temper:
we must think of some plan.

SCENA VENTIDUESIMA

SCENE 22

*Don Ottavio, Donna Anna,
Donna Elvira e detti*

*Don Ottavio, Donna Anna,
Don Elvira and the above*

LEPORELLO
Venite pur avanti,
vezzose mascherette.

LEPORELLO
Pray come this way,
fair maskers!

GIOVANNI
È aperto a tutti quanti.
Viva la libertà!

GIOVANNI
A welcome to you all.
Let freedom reign!

TUTTI
Viva la libertà!

ALL
Let freedom reign!

ANNA, ELVIRA ED OTTAVIO
Siam grati a tanti segni
di generosità.

ANNA, ELVIRA AND OTTAVIO
We thank you
for your kindly greeting.

GIOVANNI
Ricominciate il suono.
(a Leporello)
Tu accoppia i ballerini.
*(Don Ottavio balla il Minuetto
con Donna Anna)*

GIOVANNI
Strike up the band again!
(to Leporello)
Find everyone a partner.
*(Don Ottavio dances the minuet
with Donna Anna)*

LEPORELLO
Da bravi, via, ballate.

LEPORELLO
Come and dance, everyone!

(ballano)

(they dance)

ELVIRA
(a Donna Anna)
Quella è la contadina.

ELVIRA
(to Donna Anna)
That girl there's Zerlina.

63

ANNA
(a Don Ottavio)
Io moro!

OTTAVIO
(a Donna Anna)
Simulate.

LEPORELLO E MASETTO
(con ironia)
Va bene, in verità!

GIOVANNI
(a Leporello)
A bada tien Masetto.
(a Zerlina)
Il tuo compagno io sono,
Zerlina, vien pur qua . . .

*(si mette a ballare una
Contraddànza con Zerlina)*

LEPORELLO
(fa ballare a forza Masetto)
Non balli, poveretto?
Vien qua, Masetto caro,
facciam quel ch'altri fa.

MASETTO
No, no, ballar non voglio.

LEPORELLO
Eh! balla, amico mio.

ANNA
(a Don Ottavio)
Resister non poss'io!

ELVIRA ED OTTAVIO
(a Donna Anna)
Fingete, per pietà.

GIOVANNI
(ballando conduce via Zerlina)
Vieni con me, mia vita . . .

ZERLINA
Oh Numi! son tradita!

MASETTO
Lasciami . . . Ah . . . no . . . Zerlina!

ANNA
(to Don Ottavio)
I tremble!

OTTAVIO
(to Donna Anna)
Keep up your part!

LEPORELLO AND MASETTO
(ironically)
All's going very well.

GIOVANNI
(to Leporello)
Keep Masetto occupied.
(to Zerlina)
Zerlina, come this way:
I'll be your partner.

*(begins to dance the contredanse
with Zerlina)*

LEPORELLO
(forcing Masetto to dance)
Masetto, aren't you dancing?
Come on, my friend,
and join the others.

MASETTO
No, no, I'm not dancing.

LEPORELLO
Oh, come and dance, my friend.

ANNA
(to Don Ottavio)
I can hold out no longer!

ELVIRA AND OTTAVIO
(to Donna Anna)
You must keep up your part!

GIOVANNI
(dancing Zerlina away)
Come this way, my dearest . . .

ZERLINA
Oh heavens! I'm undone!

MASETTO
Let me go! Let go! . . . Zerlina!

(entra sciogliendosi da Leporello)

LEPORELLO
(tra sé)
Qui nasce una ruina.

ANNA, ELVIRA ED OTTAVIO
(fra loro)
L'iniquo da se stesso nel laccio
se ne va.

ZERLINA
(di dentro)
Gente! . . . aiuto! . . . aiuto! gente!

ANNA, ELVIRA ED OTTAVIO
Soccorriamo l'innocente . . .

(i suonatori partono)

MASETTO
Ah! Zerlina! . . .

ZERLINA
(di dentro, dalla parte opposta)
Scellerato!

ANNA, ELVIRA ED OTTAVIO
Ora grida da quel lato . . .
Ah! gettiamo giù la porta . . .

ZERLINA
Soccorretemi, o son morta!

ANNA, ELVIRA, OTTAVIO E MASETTO
Siam qui noi per tua difesa.

GIOVANNI
*(esce colla spada in mano,
conducendo per un braccio
Leporello, e finge di non
poterla sguainare per ferirlo)*
Ecco il birbo che t'ha offesa,
ma da me la pena avrà.
Mori, iniquo!

LEPORELLO
Ah! cosa fate?

GIOVANNI
Mori, dico

(freeing himself from Leporello)

LEPORELLO
(aside)
The fat is in the fire now.

ANNA, ELVIRA AND OTTAVIO
(aside)
The villain has walked into his
own trap.

ZERLINA
(from within)
Help! help! come quickly!

ANNA, ELVIRA AND OTTAVIO
We must haste to save her.

(the bands go out)

MASETTO
Oh, Zerlina!

ZERLINA
(from within, on the other side)
You traitor!

ANNA, ELVIRA AND OTTAVIO
Her cry came from there . . .
We must break down the door.

ZERLINA
Quick! Help me, or I'm ruined!

ANNA, ELVIRA, OTTAVIO AND MASETTO
We are here to defend you.

GIOVANNI
*(coming out with a sword in his hand,
holding Leporello by the arm but
pretending not to be able to
unsheath his sword to strike him)*
Here's the ruffian who attacked you;
but he must reckon with me.
Die, villain!

LEPORELLO
My lord, have mercy!

GIOVANNI
Die, I say!

OTTAVIO
(cavando una pistola)
Nol sperate . . .

ANNA, ELVIRA ED OTTAVIO
(tra loro)
L'empio crede con tal frode
di nasconder l'empietà.
(si cavano la maschera)

GIOVANNI
Donna Elvira!

ELVIRA
Si, malvagio!

GIOVANNI
Don Ottavio!

OTTAVIO
Si, signore!

GIOVANNI
(a Donna Anna)
Ah! credete . . .

ANNA
Traditore!

ZERLINA E MASETTO
Tutto, tutto già si sa.

TUTTI
(fuorché Don Giovanni e Leporello)
Trema, trema, scellerato,
saprà tosto il mondo intero
il misfatto orrendo e nero,
la tua fiera crudeltà.
Odi il tuon della vendetta
che ti fischia intorno, intorno;
sul tuo capo in questo giorno
il suo fulmine cadrà.

GIOVANNI
Non so più che quel ch'io mi faccia,
è confusa la mia testa,
e un'orribile tempesta
minacciando, oh Dio, mi va!
Ma non manca in me coraggio,
non mi perdo o mi confondo:
se cadesse ancora il mondo
nulla mai temer mi fa.

OTTAVIO
(taking out a pistol)
Not so fast, sir!

ANNA, ELVIRA AND OTTAVIO
(aside)
The scoundrel thinks by such a trick
to hide his crime.
(they unmask)

GIOVANNI
Donna Elvira!

ELVIRA
Yes, villain!

GIOVANNI
Don Ottavio!

OTTAVIO
Yes, 'tis I, sir!

GIOVANNI
(to Donna Anna)
On my honour . . .

ANNA
Traitor!

ZERLINA AND MASETTO
All your guilt is known.

ALL
(except Don Giovanni and Leporello)
Tremble, vile seducer!
All the world shall know
your base and hideous crimes,
your heartless cruelty.
Hear the thunder of vengeance
break all about you.
This day on your head
the blow shall fall.

GIOVANNI
I know not what to do,
my head is in a whirl;
a fearful storm threatens me.
But I'll not hesitate or weaken
or show the slightest fear,
though heaven itself
should fall!

LEPORELLO

Non sa più che quel ch' ei si faccia,
è confusa la sua testa,
e un'orribile tempesta
minacciando, oh Dio, lo va!
Ma non manca in lui coraggio,
non si perde, o si confonde:
se cadesse ancora il mondo
nulla mai temer lo fa.

LEPORELLO

He knows not what to do,
his head is in a whirl:
a fearful storm threatens him.
But he'll not hesitate or weaken
or show the slightest fear,
though heaven itself
should fall!

Atto secondo   Act two

SCENA PRIMA

Strada; a lato la casa di Donna
Elvira con un balcone.
Don Giovanni e Leporello

14.   DUETTO

GIOVANNI
Eh via, buffone, non mi seccar.

LEPORELLO
No, no, padrone, non vo'restar.

GIOVANNI
Sentimi, amico . . .

LEPORELLO
Vo'andar, vi dico.

GIOVANNI
Ma che ti ho fatto
che vuoi lasciarmi?

LEPORELLO
Oh, niente affatto,
quasi ammazzarmi.

GIOVANNI
Va, che sei matto, fu per burlar.

LEPORELLO
Ed io non burlo, ma voglio andar.

SCENE 1

A street; At one side Donna
Elvira's house with a balcony
Don Giovanni and Leporello

14.   DUET

GIOVANNI
Now then, you rascal, do not provoke me.

LEPORELLO
No, no, my lord: I won't stay.

GIOVANNI
Listen to me . . .

LEPORELLO
I'm going, I say.

GIOVANNI
But what have I done to you,
that you're so set on leaving?

LEPORELLO
Oh, nothing at all —
only half killed me.

GIOVANNI
Don't be stupid: it was only in jest.

LEPORELLO
Well, I'm not jesting: I'm off.

69

RECITATIVO

GIOVANNI
Leporello!

LEPORELLO
Signore!

GIOVANNI
Vien qui, facciamo pace. Prendi . . .

LEPORELLO
Cosa?

GIOVANNI
(gli dà del danaro)
Quattro doppie.

LEPORELLO
Oh! sentite:
per questa volta ancora
la cerimonia accetto;
ma non vi ci avvezzate: non credete
di sedurre i miei pari,
(prendendo la borsa)
come le donne, a forza di danari.

GIOVANNI
Non parliam più di ciò.
Ti basta l'animo
di far quel ch'io ti dico?

LEPORELLO
Purché lasciam le donne.

GIOVANNI
Lasciar le donne? Pazzo!
Sai tu ch'elle per me son
necessarie più del pan che mangio,
più dell'aria che spiro!

LEPORELLO
E avete core
d'ingannarle poi tutte?

GIOVANNI
È tutto amore.
Chi a una sola e fedele,
verso l'altre e crudele.
Io, che in me sento
si esteso sentimento,

RECITATIVE

GIOVANNI
Leporello!

LEPORELLO
Sir?

GIOVANNI
Come here; this will make peace. Take it .

LEPORELLO
What?

GIOVANNI
(giving him money)
Four gold pieces.

LEPORELLO
Oh well . . .
I'll accept the routine
just this once more;
but don't rely on it.
(taking the purse)
Don't think you can seduce a man
like me with money, as you do women.

GIOVANNI
That's enough of that!
Are you minded now
to carry out my orders?

LEPORELLO
So long as you leave women alone.

GIOVANNI
Leave women alone! You're mad!
Why, they're more necessary to me
than the bread I eat,
than the air I breathe!

LEPORELLO
And you've the heart
to deceive the lot?

GIOVANNI
It's all for love!
To be faithful to one
is to be faithless to the others.
I have so generous a heart
that I love

vo' bene a tutte quante.
Le donne poi, che calcolar non sanno,
il mio buon natural chiaman inganno.

every single one of them;
but women, who have no
head for figures, call my
good nature deception.

LEPORELLO
No ho veduto mai
naturale più vasto e più benigno.
Orsù, cosa vorreste?

LEPORELLO
I've never seen a heart
so all-embracing.
Well, what do you want of me?

GIOVANNI
Odi. Vedesti tu la cameriera
di Donna Elvira?

GIOVANNI
Listen. Did you observe
Donna Elvira's maidservant?

LEPORELLO
Io! No!

LEPORELLO
Not I.

GIOVANNI
Non hai veduto qualche cosa di
bello, caro il mio Leporello! Or io
con lei vo' tentar la mia sorte, ed
ho pensato giacché siam verso sera,
per aguzzarle meglio l'appetito,
di presentarmi a lei col tuo vestito.

GIOVANNI
Then you missed
a rare beauty, my worthy Leporello.
I'm off to try my luck with her,
and since it's getting dark now,
I thought I'd salt the jest
if I presented myself in your cloak.

LEPORELLO
E perché non potreste
presentarvi col vostro?

LEPORELLO
And why not
in your own?

GIOVANNI
Han poco credito con gente
di tal rango gli abiti signorili.
(si cava il mantello)
Sbrigati, via.

GIOVANNI
People of her station are apt to be
suspicious of a gentleman's appearance.
(taking off his own cloak)
Quick, off with it!

LEPORELLO
Signor, per più ragioni . . .

LEPORELLO
My lord, for several reasons . . .

GIOVANNI
(con collera)
Finiscila; non soffro opposizioni.

GIOVANNI
(angrily)
Have done! I'll brook no opposition.

*(fanno cambio del mantello e
del cappello)*

*(they exchange cloaks
and hats)*

SCENA SECONDA

SCENE 2

*Don Giovanni, Leporello e Donna
Elvira sul balcone.
Si fa notte a poco a poco.*

*Don Giovanni, Leporello and Donna
Elvira on the balcony.
It is gradually getting dark.*

15. TERZETTO

ELVIRA
Ah! taci, ingiusto core,
non palpitarmi in seno;
è un empio, è un traditore,
è colpa aver pietà.

LEPORELLO
(sotto voce)
Zitto . . . di Donna Elvira,
signor, la voce io sento.

GIOVANNI
(sotto voce)
Cogliere io vo' il momento.
Tu fermati un po' là.
(si mette dietro Leporello, forte)
Elvira, idolo mio!

ELVIRA
Non è costui l'ingrato?

GIOVANNI
Sì, vita mia, son io,
e chiedo carità.

ELVIRA
(tra sé)
Numi, che strano affetto
mi si risveglia in petto!

LEPORELLO
(tra sé)
State a veder la pazza,
che ancor gli crederà!

GIOVANNI
Discendi, o gioia bella!
Vedrai che tu sei quella
che adora l'alma mia:
pentito io sono già.

ELVIRA
No, non ti credo, o barbaro.

GIOVANNI
(con trasporto e quasi piangendo)
Ah, credimi, o m'uccido.

15. TRIO

ELVIRA
Be still, fickle heart,
and cease to agitate my breast:
he is a wicked betrayer;
to pity him is a sin.

LEPORELLO
(sotto voce)
Softly, my lord . . .
I heard the voice of Donna Elvira.

GIOVANNI
(sotto voce)
Then I'll seize the moment.
Stand here before me.
(aloud, standing behind Leporello)
My adored Elvira!

ELVIRA
Is that not the deceiver?

GIOVANNI
Yes, 'tis I my heart,
and seeking your forgiveness.

ELVIRA
(aside)
Heavens, what strange emotion
awakens in my bosom!

LEPORELLO
(aside)
She must be mad indeed
to trust in him again!

GIOVANNI
Come down, joy of my life!
You are the one my soul adores,
and I am penitent.

ELVIRA
You brute, I don't believe you!

GIOVANNI
(agitatedly, as if in tears)
You must believe me, or I'll kill myself.

LEPORELLO
(sotto voce)
Se seguitate, io rido.

GIOVANNI
Idolo mio, vien qua.

ELVIRA
(tra sé)
Dei, che cimento è questo!
Non so s'io vado o resto . . .
Ah! proteggete voi
la mia credulità.
(Donna Elvira parte dal balcone)

GIOVANNI
(tra sé)
Spero che cada presto;
che bel colpetto è questo!
Più fertile talento
del mio, no, non si dà.

LEPORELLO
(tra sé)
Gia quel mendace labbro
torna a sedur costei;
deh, proteggete, o Dei,
la sua credulità.

RECITATIVO

GIOVANNI
(allegrissimo)
Amico, che ti par?

LEPORELLO .
Mi par che abbiate
un'anima di bronzo

GIOVANNI
Va là che se' il gran gonzo.
Ascolta bene:
quando costei qui viene,
tu corri ad abbracciarla,
falle quattro carezze,
fingi la voce mia; poi con bell'arte
cerca teco condurla in altra parte.

LEPORELLO
Ma signor . . .

LEPORELLO
(sotto voce)
If this goes on, I'll laugh aloud.

GIOVANNI
Come down, my dearest.

ELVIRA
(aside)
I'm torn asunder:
I know not if to go or no . . .
Ye gods, protect my trusting heart!

(she leaves the balcony)

GIOVANNI
(aside)
I hope she'll give in quickly:
that would be sport indeed!
There's none cleverer than I
at such delicious jests.

LEPORELLO
(aside)
His lying tongue
soon tempts her:
ye gods, protect
her trusting heart!

RECITATIVE

GIOVANNI
(in high spirits)
Well, what do you think of that?

LEPORELLO
I think you have
a heart of stone.

GIOVANNI
I think you're a blockhead . . .
Now listen:
when she appears,
run and embrace her;
don't stint your caresses,
imitate my voice: then do your best
to get her away somewhere.

LEPORELLO
But sir . . .

73

GIOVANNI
Non più repliche.

LEPORELLO
E se poi mi conosce?

GIOVANNI
Non ti conoscerà, se tu non vuoi.
Zitto: ell'apre; giudizio.

(va in disparte)

SCENA TERZA

Donna Elvira e detti

ELVIRA
Eccomi a voi.

GIOVANNI
(tra sé)
Veggiamo che farà.

LEPORELLO
(tra sé)
Che imbroglio!

ELVIRA
(a Leporello)
Dunque creder potrò che i pianti
miei abbian vinto quel cor? Dunque
pentito l'amato Don Giovanni al
suo dovere e all'amor mio ritorna?

LEPORELLO
(alterando sempre la voce)
Sì, carina!

ELVIRA
Crudele! se sapeste
quante lacrime e quanti
sospir voi mi costaste!

LEPORELLO
Io? vita mia!

ELVIRA
Voi.

GIOVANNI
No more objections!

LEPORELLO
Suppose she recognises me?

GIOVANNI
She won't, unless you let her.
Hush! she's coming. Be careful now!

(he withdraws)

SCENE 3

Donna Elvira and the above

ELVIRA
Here I am, then.

GIOVANNI
(aside)
Let's see what she does.

LEPORELLO
(aside)
Here's a fine to-do!

ELVIRA
(to Leporello)
Can I believe my tears have melted
your heart? And that my
beloved Giovanni has repented and
returned to his obligations and his love?

LEPORELLO
(disguising his voice)
Yes, my dearest!

ELVIRA
Cruel one! if you knew
the tears and sighs
that you have caused me!

LEPORELLO
I, dear heart?

ELVIRA
Yes, you.

74

LEPORELLO
Poverina! quanto mi dispiace!

ELVIRA
Non fuggirete più?

LEPORELLO
No, muso bello.

ELVIRA
Sarete sempre mio?

LEPORELLO
Sempre.

ELVIRA
Carissimo!

LEPORELLO
Carissima!
(tra sé)
La burla mi dà gusto.

ELVIRA
Mio tesoro!

LEPORELLO
Mia Venere!

ELVIRA
Son per voi tutta fuoco.

LEPORELLO
Io tutto cenere.

GIOVANNI
(tra sé)
Il birbo si riscalda.

ELVIRA
E non m'ingannerete?

LEPORELLO
No, sicuro.

ELVIRA
Giuratelo.

LEPORELLO
Lo giuro a questa mano,
che bacio con trasporto,

LEPORELLO
Poor darling! I'm deeply sorry.

ELVIRA
You won't leave me again?

LEPORELLO
No, my fairest.

ELVIRA
You'll be mine always?

LEPORELLO
Always.

ELVIRA
My dearest!

LEPORELLO
My darling!
(aside)
I'm beginning to enjoy this.

ELVIRA
My beloved!

LEPORELLO
My Venus!

ELVIRA
I am on fire for you.

LEPORELLO
I'm burnt to ashes.

GIOVANNI
(aside)
The rascal's warming up!

ELVIRA
And you will not deceive me?

LEPORELLO
No, never.

ELVIRA
Swear it.

LEPORELLO
I swear it by this hand
I cover with kisses,

a que'bei lumi . . .

GIOVANNI
(fingendo di uccidere qualcheduno)
Ah! eh! ih! ah! ih! ah! sei morto . . .

ELVIRA E LEPORELLO
Oh Numi!

(fuggon assieme)

GIOVANNI
(ridendo)
Ih! oh! par che la sorte
mi secondi. Veggiamo:
la finestre son queste. Ora cantiamo.

16.   CANZONETTA

GIOVANNI
*(canta accompagnandosi col
mandolino)*
Deh! vieni alla finestra, o mio tesoro.
Deh, vieni a consolar il pianto mio.
Se neghi a me di dar qualche ristoro,
davanti agli occhi tuo morir vogl'io.
Tu ch'hai la bocca dolce più del miele,
tu che il zucchero porti in mezzo al core,
non esser, gioia mia, con me crudele,
lasciati almen vedere, o bell'amore!

SCENA QUARTA

*Masetto, armato d'archibuso
e pistola, Contadini e detto*

RECITATIVO

GIOVANNI
V'è gente alla finestra:
forse è dessa.
Zi zi . . .

MASETTO
*(ai contadini armati di
fucili e bastoni)*
Non ci stanchiam, amici.
Il cor mi dice
che trovarlo dobbiam.

and by those orbs . . .

GIOVANNI
(pretending to attack them)
Stand and deliver!

ELVIRA AND LEPORELLO
Heaven protect us!

(they both fly)

GIOVANNI
(laughing)
It seems my luck is turning.
Let's see: this is the window:
I'll serenade her.

16.   SERENADE

GIOVANNI
*(accompanying himself on the
mandoline)*
O come to your window, beloved;
O come and dispel all my sorrow!
If you refuse me some solace,
before your dear eyes I will die.
Your lips are sweeter than
honey, your heart is sweetness
itself: then be not cruel, my
angel: I beg for one glance,
my beloved!

SCENE 4

*Masetto, armed with arquebus
and pistol, villagers and the above*

RECITATIVE

GIOVANNI
There's someone at the window:
it must be she.
Pst, pst . . .

MASETTO
*(to the villagers, armed with guns
and sticks)*
Don't weaken, my friends.
I'm positive
we'll find him.

GIOVANNI
(tra sé)
Qualcuno parla.

MASETTO
(ai contadini)
Fermatevi; mi pare
che alcuno qui si muova.

GIOVANNI
(tra sé)
Se non fallo, è Masetto.

MASETTO
(forte)
Chi va la?
(ai suoi)
Non risponde.
Animo, schioppo al muso:
(più forte)
chi va la?

GIOVANNI
(tra sé)
Non è solo:
ci vuol giudizio.
(forte)
Amici . . .
(piano)
Non mi voglio scoprir.
(cerca d'imitar la voce di Leporello)
Sei tu, Masetto?

MASETTO
(in collera)
Appunto quello. E tu?

GIOVANNI
Non mi conosci? Il servo
son io di Don Giovanni.

MASETTO
Leporello!
Servo di quell'indegno cavaliere!

GIOVANNI
Certo, di quel briccone.

MASETTO
Di quell'uomo senza onore!
Ah, dimmi un poco,

GIOVANNI
(aside)
Somebody is speaking.

MASETTO
(to the villagers)
Wait a moment: I thought
I heard someone move.

GIOVANNI
(aside)
That's surely Masetto!

MASETTO
(aloud)
Who's there?
(to his friends)
No answer.
Courage! Have your weapons ready.
(more loudly)
Who's there?

GIOVANNI
(aside)
He's not alone:
I must be careful.
(aloud)
Friends!
(aside)
I mustn't be found out.
(trying to imitate Leporello's voice)
Is that you, Masetto?

MASETTO
(angrily)
That's me all right. Who are you?

GIOVANNI
Don't you know me?
I'm Don Giovanni's servant.

MASETTO
Leporello!
The servant of that worthless lord!

GIOVANNI
Just so, of that scoundrel.

MASETTO
Of that dishonourable man!
Ah then, can you tell me

dove possiam trovarlo?	where we can find him?
Lo cerco con costor per trucidarlo.	Me and my friends are out to kill him.

GIOVANNI
(piano)
Bagatelle!
(forte)
Bravissimo, Masetto,
anch'io con voi m'unisco,
per fargliela a quel birbo di padrone
Or senti un po' qual è la mia intenzione.

GIOVANNI
(softly)
Puny threat!
(aloud)
My worthy Masetto, I'll join with you
and get my own back
on my rogue of a
master. But listen: I have
a plan.

17. ARIA

GIOVANNI
Metà di voi qua vadano,
(accennando a dèstra)
e gli altri vadan là,
(accennando a sinistra)
e pian pianin lo cerchino,
lontan non fia di qua.
Se un uom e una ragazza
passeggian per la piazza,
se sotto a una finestra
fare all'amor sentite,
ferite pur, ferite,
il mio padron sarà!
In testa egli ha un cappello
con candidi pennacchi.
Addosso un gran mantello
e spada al fianco egli ha.
(ai contadini)
Andate, fate presto!
(a Masetto)
Tu sol verrai con me.
Noi far dobbiamo il resto
e già vedrai cos'è.

17. ARIA

GIOVANNI
Let half of you go this way,
(pointing to the right)
the other half go that,
(pointing to the left)
but treading very cautiously:
he can't be far from here.
If you see a man with a maid
on the street
or making love
beneath a window,
then strike out hard:
it's bound to be my master!
He's wearing a big hat
with white plumes on his head,
a cloak around him
and a sword at his side.
(to the villagers)
Be quick and go about it!
(to Masetto)
You alone shall come with me.
We can deal with the rest —
and how, you soon shall see.

(Partono i contadini da opposte vie)   *(the villagers exeunt severally)*

SCENA QUINTA

Don Giovanni, Masetto

RECITATIVO

GIOVANNI
Zitto, Lascia ch'io senta . . .
Ottimamente.

SCENE V

Don Giovanni and Masetto

RECITATIVE

GIOVANNI
Hush! Let me listen . . .
All's well.

essendosi assicurato che i contadini sono già lontani)	*(having assured himself that the villagers are far away)*
Dunque dobbiam ucciderlo?	So we ought to kill him?
MASETTO	MASETTO
Sicuro.	Indeed yes.
GIOVANNI	GIOVANNI
E non ti basteria rompergli l'ossa, fracassargli le spalle?	It wouldn't be enough to give him a good thrashing or break his ribs?
MASETTO	MASETTO
No, no; voglio ammazzarlo, vo' farlo in cento brani.	No, no, I'm going to massacre him, make mincemeat of him.
GIOVANNI	GIOVANNI
Hai buone armi?	Are you well armed?
MASETTO	MASETTO
Cospetto! Ho pria questo moschetto, e poi questa pistola.	Just look! Here I've a musket, and a pistol besides.
(dà moschetto e pistola a Don Giovanni)	*(shows them to Don Giovanni)*
GIOVANNI	GIOVANNI
E poi?	What else?
MASETTO	MASETTO
Non basta?	Isn't that enough?
GIOVANNI	GIOVANNI
Eh! basta certo. Or prendi: *(batte Masetto col rovescio della spada)* questa, per la pistola, questa, per il moschetto.	Oh, plenty. Well then: *(beating Masetto with the flat of his sword)* take that for the pistol, and that for the musket ...
MASETTO	MASETTO
Ahi, ahi! soccorso!	Oh, oh! help!
GIOVANNI	GIOVANNI
Taci, o t'uccido. Questa, per ammazzarlo, questa, per farlo in brani. Villano! mascalzon! ceffo da cani!	Quiet, or I'll kill you! That's for massacring him, and that's for making mincemeat of him. You knave! you blackguard! you dog!
(Masetto cade e Don Giovanni parte)	*(Masetto falls down and Don Giovanni goes off)*

SCENA SESTA

Masetto, indi Zerlina con lanterna

MASETTO
(gridando forte)
Ahi! ahi! la testa mia!
Ahi! ahi! le spalle e il petto!

ZERLINA
Di sentire mi parve la voce
di Masetto.

MASETTO
Oh Dio! Zerlina mia, soccorso.

ZERLINA
Cos'è stato?

MASETTO
L'iniquo, il scellerato
mi ruppe l'ossa e i nervi.

ZERLINA
Oh poveretta me! Chi?

MASETTO
Leporello,
o qualche diavol che somiglia a lui.

ZERLINA
Crudel! non tel diss'io
che con questa tua pazza gelosia
ti ridurresti a qualche brutto passo?
Dove ti duole?

MASETTO
Qui.

ZERLINA
E poi?

MASETTO
Qui ancora.

ZERLINA
E poi non ti duol altro?

MASETTO
Duolmi un poco questo pie',
questo braccio e questa mano.

SCENE 6

Masetto, then Zerlina with a lantern

MASETTO
(groaning loudly)
Oh, oh! my head!
Oh, oh! my back, my shoulders!

ZERLINA
I thought I heard Masetto's
voice.

MASETTO
O Zerlina, dear Zerlina! Help me!

ZERLINA
What's happened?

MASETTO
The villain, the ruffian
has broken every bone in my body.

ZERLINA
My poor darling! Who?

MASETTO
Leporello,
or some fiend in his shape.

ZERLINA
The brute! Didn't I tell you
that your stupid jealousy
would land you in some trouble?
Where does it hurt?

MASETTO
Here.

ZERLINA
Where else?

MASETTO
Here, and here too.

ZERLINA
Doesn't it hurt anywhere else?

MASETTO
My foot hurts a bit, and my arm,
and this hand.

ZERLINA
Via, via, non è gran mal,
e il resto è sano.
Vientene meco a casa:
purché tu mi prometta
d'essere men geloso,
io, io ti guarirò, caro il mio sposo.

8. ARIA

ZERLINA
Vedrai, carino,
se sei buonino,
che bel rimedio
ti voglio dar.
È naturale,
non dà disgusto,
e lo speziale non lo sa far.
È un certo balsamo
che porto addosso,
dare tel posso
se il vuo provar.
Saper vorresti
dove mi sta;
sentilo battere,
toccami qua.

*(gli fa toccare il cuore,
poi partono)*

SCENA SETTIMA

*Atrio oscuro con tre porte in casa
di Donna Anna.
Donna Elvira e Leporello*

RECITATIVO

LEPORELLO
(fingendo la voce del padrone)
Di molte faci il lume
s'avvicina, o mio ben; stiamo qui
un poco finché da noi si scosta.

ELVIRA
Ma che temi,
adorato mio sposo?

LEPORELLO
Nulla, nulla . . .

ZERLINA
Come, come, it's not so bad,
if the rest of you's all right.
Come home with me;
and if you promise not to be
so jealous again, I'll make you
better, my dear husband.

18. ARIA

ZERLINA
If you'll be good, my dear,
you'll see
the cure I have for you!
I know you'll like it;
it's nature's cure,
though no apothecary
can prescribe it.
It's a certain balm
I carry within me
which I can give you,
if you'll try it.
If you want to know
where I keep it,
then feel it beating
put your hand here.

*(lays his hand on her heart,
then they go off)*

SCENE 7

*A dark courtyard with three doors,
before Donna Anna's house.
Donna Elvira and Leporello*

RECITATIVE

LEPORELLO
(assuming his master's voice)
I see the light of many torches
coming this way, my dear: let's stay
out of sight until they're past.

ELVIRA
But, my adored one,
what is there to fear?

LEPORELLO
Nothing, nothing . . .

Certi riguardi . . . lo vo' veder
se il lume è già lontano.
(tra sé)
Ah, come da costei liberarmi?
(forte)
Rimanti, anima bella.

ELVIRA
Ah! non lasciarmi.

19. SESTETTO

ELVIRA
Sola, sola in buio loco,
palpitar il cor mi sento,
e m'assale un tal spavento
che mi sembra di morir.

LEPORELLO
(andando a tentone, tra sé)
Più che cerco, men ritrovo
questa porta sciagurata . . .
Piano, piano, l'ho trovata:
ecco il tempo di fuggir.

(sbaglia l'uscita)

SCENA OTTAVA

*Donna Anna, Don Ottavio,
vestiti a lutto. Servi con
lumi, e detti.
Donna Elvira al venire dei
lumi si ritira in un angolo,
Leporello in un altro.*

OTTAVIO
Tergi il ciglio, o vita mia!
e dà calma al tuo dolore;
l'ombra omai del genitore
pena avrà de' tuoi martir.

ANNA
Lascia almen alla mia pena
questo piccolo ristoro;
sol la morte, o mio tesoro,
il mio pianto può finir.

ELVIRA
(piano, senza esser vista)
Ah! dov'è lo sposo mio?

but it might be prudent . . .
I'll go and see if the lights are moving awa
(aside)
How can I get rid of her?
(aloud)
Stay here, my love . . .

ELVIRA
Oh do not leave me!

19. SEXTET

ELVIRA
All alone in this dark spot
I feel my heart is throbbing
and such fear overcomes me
that death itself seems near.

LEPORELLO
(aside, groping)
The more I search, the less I find
this confounded doorway!
Softly though, I've found it:
now's the time to get away.

(mistakes the way out)

SCENE 8

*Donna Anna and Don Ottavio,
both in mourning, servants with
lights, and the above.
At the approach of lights Donna
Elvira retires into one corner,
Leporello into another.*

OTTAVIO
Cease your weeping, my beloved,
and still your sorrow;
your father's shade would grieve
to see your anguish.

ANNA
Leave me but this small relief
for my sorrow, my dearest:
only death can end my pain.

ELVIRA
(softly, still unseen)
Ah, where has my husband gone?

LEPORELLO *(dalla porta, senza esser visto, piano)* Se mi trovan, son perduto.	**LEPORELLO** *(from the door, unseen, softly)* If she finds me I'm done for!
ELVIRA E LEPORELLO Una porta là vegg'io. Cheta (o), cheta (o), io vo'partir.	**ELVIRA E LEPORELLO** I see a doorway here. I'll slip quietly away.
(Leporello,nell'uscire, s'incontra con Masetto e Zerlina)	*(as Leporello goes out he runs into Masetto and Zerlina)*

SCENA NONA / SCENE 9

Masetto con bastone, Zerlina e detti	*Masetto with a big stick, Zerlina and the above*
ZERLINA E MASETTO Ferma, briccone! Dove ten vai? *(Leporello s'asconde la faccia)*	**ZERLINA AND MASETTO** Wretch, now we've caught you! Where are you off to? *(Leporello hides his face)*
ANNA ED OTTAVIO Ecco il fellone . . . Com'era qua?	**ANNA AND OTTAVIO** Here's the villain! How came he here?
ANNA, ZERLINA, OTTAVIO E MASETTO Ah! mora il perfido che m'ha tradito.	**ANNA, ZERLINA, OTTAVIO AND MASETTO** Death to the betrayer!
ELVIRA É mio marito . . . Pietà! pietà!	**ELVIRA** He is my husband . . . Have mercy!
ANNA, ZERLINA, OTTAVIO E MASETTO É Donna Elvira quella ch'io vedo? Appena il credo . . . No, no, morrà!	**ANNA, ZERLINA, OTTAVIO AND MASETTO** Is this Donna Elvira I see? I can't believe it . . . No, he shall die!
(Mentre Don Ottavio sta per ucciderlo, Leporello si scopre e si mette in ginocchio.)	*(As Don Ottavio goes to kill him, Leporello reveals himself and falls to his knees)*
LEPORELLO *(quasi piangendo)* Perdon, perdono, signori miei: quello io non sono, sbaglia costei. Viver lasciatemi, per carità!	**LEPORELLO** *(almost in tears)* O spare me, spare me! I'm not your man . . . she is mistaken. Spare my life, I beg you.
GLI ALTRI Dei! Leporello! Che inganno è questo? Stupido (a) resto!	**THE OTHERS** What! Leporello! And in disguise too! I am amazed.

83

Che mai sarà?

What now?

LEPORELLO
(tra sé)
Mille torbidi pensieri
mi s'aggiran per la testa;
se mi salvo in tal tempesta
è un prodigio in verità.

LEPORELLO
(aside)
A thousand desperate thoughts
are whirling in my head:
if I survive this storm
'twill be a miracle indeed.

GLI ALTRI
(tra loro)
Mille torbidi pensieri
mi s'aggiran per la testa;
Che giornata, o stelle, è questa!
Che impensata novità!

THE OTHERS
(aside)
A thousand desperate thoughts
are whirling in my head.
Heavens, what a day of
shocks this is!

(Donna Anna parte coi servi)

(exit Donna Anna with the servants)

RECITATIVO

RECITATIVE

ZERLINA
(a Leporello, con furia)
Dunque quello sei tu che il mio
Masetto poco fa crudelmente
maltrattasti.

ZERLINA
(furiously, to Leporello)
So it was you who cruelly
beat my poor Masetto just
before.

ELVIRA
Dunque tu m'ingannasti, o
scellerato, spacciandoti con me
per Don Giovanni?

ELVIRA
So you deceived me, wretch,
by passing yourself off as
Don Giovanni?

OTTAVIO
Dunque tu in questi panni
venisti qui per qualche tradimento.

OTTAVIO
So you came here in these garments
for some mischief!

ELVIRA
A me tocca punirlo . . .

ELVIRA
Let me be the one to chastise him.

ZERLINA
Anzi a me.

ZERLINA
No, rather me.

OTTAVIO
No, no, a me.

OTTAVIO
No, no, I will.

MASETTO
Accoppatelo meco tutti tre.

MASETTO
Let's all three beat him together.

20. ARIA

20. ARIA

LEPORELLO
Ah! pietà, signori miei!

LEPORELLO
Oh spare me, good people!

Do ragione a voi . . . a lei . . .	You are right, sir . . . and so are you,
Ma il delitto mio non è.	ma'am . . . but the real fault isn't mine.
Il padron con prepotenza	'Twas by my master's doing
l'innocenza mi rubò.	that I was led astray.
(piano a Donna Elvira)	*(softly to Donna Elvira)*
Donna Elvira! compatite;	Donna Elvira! forgive me:
già capite come andò.	you know how he is.
(a Zerlina)	*(to Zerlina)*
Di Masetto non so nulla,	About Masetto I know nothing,
(accennando Donna Elvira)	*(indicating Donna Elvira)*
nel dirà questa fanciulla;	as this lady here can vouch;
è un'oretta circum circa	for nearly an hour
che non lei girando vo.	I've been walking back and forth with her.
(a Don Ottavio, con confusione)	*(to Don Ottavio, in confusion)*
A voi, signore, non dico niente.	To you, sir, I can say nothing . . .
Certo timore . . . certo accidente . . .	It was partly fear and partly accident . . .
Di fuori chiaro . . . di dentro scuro . . .	it was light outside but dark
Non c'è riparo . . . la porta, il muro . . .	in here . . . I've no excuse . . .
	the door, the wall . . .
(additando la porta dov'erasi	*(pointing to the door which had*
chiuso per errore)	*kept him in)*
Io me ne vo da quel lato . . .	and I was just on that side . . .
Poi qui celato, l'affar si sa . . .	so I hid in here, and the rest you know . . .
Ma s'io sapeva, fuggia per qua! . . .	But if I'd known, I'd have run from here!
(fugge precipitosamente)	*(rushes out)*

SCENA DECIMA

SCENE 10

Don Ottavio, Donna Elvira,
Zerlina e Masetto

Don Ottavio, Donna Elvira,
Zerlina and Masetto

RECITATIVO

RECITATIVE

ELVIRA
Ferma, perfido; ferma.

ELVIRA
Stop, villain, stop!

MASETTO
Il birbo ha l'ali ai piedi.

MASETTO
The rogue's got wings on his feet.

ZERLINA
Con qual arte si sottrasse l'iniquo!

ZERLINA
How neatly he got away!

OTTAVIO
Amici miei! Dopo eccessi si
enormi, dubitar non possiam che
Don Giovanni non sia l'empio uccisore
del padre di Donna Anna; in questa
casa per poche ore fermatevi: un

OTTAVIO
Friends, after the shocking events
we have witnessed, there can be no doubt
that Don Giovanni was the wicked slayer
of Donna Anna's father. Stay in this
house an hour or so: I will inform the

85

ricorso vo'far a chi si deve, e in
pochi instanti vendicarvi prometto;
così vuole dover, pietade, affetto.

authorities, and can promise you
retribution before long: honour,
compassion and affection demand as much

21. ARIA

OTTAVIO
Il mio tesoro intanto
andate a consolar:
e del bel ciglio il pianto
cercate d'asciugar.
Ditele che i suoi torti
a vendicar io vado;
che sol di stragi e morti
nunzio voglio tornar.

(partono)

21. ARIA

OTTAVIO
Meantime go and console my dearest one,
and seek to dry the tears from her
lovely eyes.
Tell her that I have gone to avenge her
wrongs, and will return only as the
messenger of punishment and death.

(exeunt)

SCENA UNDICESIMA

Donna Elvira sola

SCENE 11

Donna Elvira alone

21b. RECITATIVO ED ARIA

ELVIRA
Il quali eccessi, o Numi!
in quai misfatti orribili, tremendi,
è avvolto il sciagurato!
Ah no, non può tardar l'ira del
cielo, la giustizia tardar.
Sentir già parmi la fatale saetta,
che gli piomba sul capo!
Aperto veggio il baratro mortal.
Misera Elvira! Che contrasto
d'affetti in sen ti nasce! Perché
questi sospiri e queste ambasce?

21b. RECITATIVE AND ARIA

ELVIRA
In what enormities, O God,
in what dreadful crimes
is the wretch involved!
The wrath of Heaven must be at hand;
its justice will not tarry.
I see the deadly thunderbolt
poised above his head!
I see the fatal abyss open before him.
Unhappy Elvira, what conflicting
emotions strive in thy heart!
Why these sighs, why this distress?

ARIA

ELVIRA
Mi tradi quell'alma ingrata,
infelice, oh Dio! mi fa.
Ma tradita, abbandonata,
provo ancor per lui pietà.
Quando sento il mio tormento
di vendetta il cor favella,
ma se guardo il suo cimento
palpitando il cor mi va.

(parte)

ARIA

ELVIRA
That ungrateful man betrayed me
and left me wretched, O God!
Yet betrayed and forsaken,
still I feel pity for him.
When I think of my wrongs
my heart urges vengeance,
but when I see his peril
my heart falters within me.

(exit)

SCENA DODICESIMA

Luogo chiuso in forma di sepolcreto, con diverse statue equestri, tra le quali quella del Commendatore. Chiaro di luna. Don Giovanni, poi Leporello, la statua del Commendatore.

RECITATIVO

GIOVANNI
(ridendo, entra pel muretto.)
Ah! ah! ah! questa è buona!
Or lasciala cercar. Che bella notte!
E più chiara del giorno; sembra
fatta per gir a zonzo a caccia di
ragazze. È tardi?
(guardando l'orologio)
Oh, ancor non sono due della notte.
Avrei voglia un po' di saper com'è
finito l'affar tra Leporello e Donna
Elvira, s'egli ha avuto giudizio . . .

LEPORELLO
(si affaccia al muretto)
Alfin vuole ch'io faccia un precipizio.

GIOVANNI
(tra sé)
E desso.
(forte)
Ehi, Leporello!

LEPORELLO
Chi mi chiama?

GIOVANNI
Non conosci il padrone!

LEPORELLO
Così nol conoscessi!

GIOVANNI
Come, birbo?

LEPORELLO
Ah, siete voi? Scusate!

GIOVANNI
Cos'è stato?

SCENE 12

An enclosed churchyard with several equestrian statues, including that of the Commendatore. Moonlight. Don Giovanni, then Leporello, the statue of the Commendatore.

RECITATIVE

GIOVANNI
(laughing, jumping over the wall)
Ha, ha, ha! This is fun!
Let her look for me here!
What a lovely night: it's brighter than
day. It's just made for hunting about
for girls. Is it late?
(looking at the clock)
Oh, it's not yet two o'clock.
I'd like to know the end of the story
of Leporello and Donna Elvira,
and if he was prudent . . .

LEPORELLO
(appearing at the wall)
I'm sure he meant to see me done for.

GIOVANNI
(aside)
There he is.
(aloud)
Hey, Leporello!

LEPORELLO
Who's calling me?

GIOVANNI
Don't you know your master?

LEPORELLO
I wish I'd never met him!

GIOVANNI
What's that, rascal?

LEPORELLO
Oh, it's you! Forgive me!

GIOVANNI
What's happened?

87

LEPORELLO
Per cagion vostra io fui quasi
accoppato.

GIOVANNI
Ebben, non era questo un onore
per te?

LEPORELLO
Signor, vel dono.

GIOVANNI
Via, via, vien qua. Che belle
cose ti deggio dire!

LEPORELLO
Ma cosa fate qua?

GIOVANNI
Vien dentro e lo saprai.
Diverse storielle che accadute
mi son da che partisti, ti dirò
un'altra volta; or la più bella
ti vo' solo narrar.

LEPORELLO
Donnesca al certo.

*(Rende il cappello e il mantello
al padrone, e riprende quelli che
aveva cambiati con lui.)*

GIOVANNI
C'è dubbio? una fanciulla
bella, giovin, galante,
per la strada incontrai;
Le vado appresso, la prendo
per la man; fuggir mi vuole;
dico poche parole; ella mi piglia
sai per chi?

LEPORELLO
Non lo so.

GIOVANNI
Per Leporello.

LEPORELLO
Per me?

LEPORELLO
On your account I've been nearly
murdered.

GIOVANNI
Indeed! Quite an honour
for you!

LEPORELLO
Thank you for nothing.

GIOVANNI
Now, now, come here.
I've a pretty tale to tell you.

LEPORELLO
But what are you doing here?

GIOVANNI
Come down, and I'll tell you.
Various adventures which I've
had since you left me
I'll tell you about another time:
I'll give you just the choicest now.

LEPORELLO
It's about a woman, for sure.

*(He gives his master back his hat
and cloak and takes those he
exchanged with him.)*

GIOVANNI
What else?
I met a young girl in the street,
pretty and well dressed;
I approached her and took her hand;
she tried to run away, but I said
a word or two, and she took me for —
who do you think?

LEPORELLO
I don't know.

GIOVANNI
For Leporello.

LEPORELLO
For me?

GIOVANNI
Per te.

GIOVANNI
For you.

LEPORELLO
Va bene.

LEPORELLO
That's good!

GIOVANNI
Per la mano essa allora mi prende.

GIOVANNI
Then she it was who took me by the hand.

LEPORELLO
Ancora meglio.

LEPORELLO
Better and better!

GIOVANNI
M'accarezza, m'abbraccia.
»Caro il mio Leporello!
Leporello mio caro!«
Allora m'accorsi
ch'era qualche tua bella.

GIOVANNI
She caressed me and kissed me.
"Oh my dear Leporello!
Leporello, my darling!"
So I realised
she was one of your conquests.

LEPORELLO
(tra sé)
Oh maledetto!

LEPORELLO
(aside)
Damn him!

GIOVANNI
Dell'inganno approfitto; non so
come mi riconosce, grida,
sento gente, a fuggire mi metto,
e, pronto pronto, per quel
muretto in questo loco io monto.

GIOVANNI
I put her mistake to advantage; but
somehow she recognised me and
called out. I heard people and took
to flight, and quick as a flash climbed
the wall into this place.

LEPORELLO
E mi dite la cosa
con tanta indifferenza?

LEPORELLO
And you tell me this quite
coolly?

GIOVANNI
Perché no?

GIOVANNI
Why not?

LEPORELLO
Ma se fosse costei stata mia moglie?

LEPORELLO
Supposing she had been my wife?

GIOVANNI
(ridendo forte)
Meglio ancora!

GIOVANNI
(laughing loudly)
Better still!

COMMENDATORE
Di rider finirai pria
dell'aurora.

COMMENDATORE
Your laughter will be silenced
before morning.

GIOVANNI
Chi ha parlato?

GIOVANNI
Who spoke?

89

LEPORELLO
(estremamente impaurito)
Ah! qualche anima
sarà dell'altro mondo,
che vi conosce a fondo.

GIOVANNI
Taci, sciocco!
*(mette mano alla spada, e cerca
qua e là pel sepolcreto dando
diverse percosse alle statue ecc.)*
Chi va là? chi va là?

COMMENDATORE
Ribaldo! audace!
Lascia a' morti la pace.

LEPORELLO
(tremando)
Ve l'ho detto? . . .

GIOVANNI
(con indifferenza e sprezzo)
Sarà qualcun di fuori
che si burla di noi.
Ehi! del Commendatore
non è questa la statua?
Leggi un poco quella iscrizion.

LEPORELLO
Scusate.
Non ho imparato a leggere
ai raggi della luna.

GIOVANNI
Leggi, dico.

LEPORELLO
»Dell'empio che mi trasse al
passo estremo. Qui attendo
la vendetta.«
(a Don Giovanni)
Udiste? Io tremo!

GIOVANNI
Oh, vecchio buffonissimo!
Digli che questa sera
l'attendo a cena meco

LEPORELLO
Che pazzia! Ma vi par?

LEPORELLO
(extremely frightened)
It must have been
some spirit from the other world
who knows all about you.

GIOVANNI
Quiet, fool.
*(puts his hand to his sword, and
searches through the cemetery, striking
the monuments, etc.)*
Who's there? Who's there?

COMMENDATORE
Impudent scoundrel!
Leave the dead in peace!

LEPORELLO
(fearfully)
I told you so!

GIOVANNI
(with indifference and disdain)
It must be someone over the
wall playing a joke on us . . .
Look, isn't that the statue
of the Commendatore?
Read me the inscription.

LEPORELLO
Excuse me . . .
I never could see
to read by moonlight.

GIOVANNI
Read it, I say.

LEPORELLO
"Here I await Heaven's
vengeance upon a vile
assassin."
(to Don Giovanni)
You hear that? I tremble!

GIOVANNI
That stupid old fool!
Tell him I'll expect him
for supper with me tonight.

LEPORELLO
Are you mad? Do you think . . .?

Oh Dei! mirate
che terribili occhiate egli ci dà . . .
Par vivo . . . par che senta . . .
E che voglia parlar . . .

O God, look
at the terrible way he stares!
It's as if he were alive
and heard you, and wished to speak.

GIOVANNI
Orsù, va là. O qui t'ammazzo
e poi ti seppellisco.

GIOVANNI
Go on now, or I'll kill you
and bury you too.

LEPORELLO
Piano . . . piano . . ., signore . . .
ora ubbidisco.

LEPORELLO
Oh please, sir!
I'll do your bidding.

22. DUETTO

22. DUET

LEPORELLO
O statua gentilissima
del gran Commendatore . . .
Padron . . . mi trema il core . . .
Non pos . . . so . . . ter . . . mi . . .
nar . . .

LEPORELLO
O most noble statue
of the great Commendatore . . .
Oh, sir, I'm trembling
all over. I can't go
on . . .

GIOVANNI
Finiscila, o nel petto
ti metto quest'acciar.
(tra sé)
Che gusto! che spassetto!
Lo voglio far tremar.

GIOVANNI
Get on with it.
or my sword shall run you through.
(aside)
It's most amusing
making him tremble so!

LEPORELLO
Che impiccio! che capriccio!
Io sentomi gelar!
O statua gentilissima,
benché di marmo siate . . .
Ah! padron mio . . . mirate . . .
che seguita . . . a guardar . . .

LEPORELLO
What mad caprice!
My blood freezes!
Most noble statue,
although you are of marble . . .
Oh, sir, just look . . .
he's glaring at me.. . .

GIOVANNI
Mori . . .

GIOVANNI
Die then . . .

LEPORELLO
No, no . . . attendete . . .
(alla statua)
Signor, il padron mio . . .
badate ben . . . non io . . .
vorria con voi cenar . . .
Ah! ah; che scena è questa!
(La statua china la testa)
Oh ciel! . . . chinò la testa . . .

LEPORELLO
No, no . . . wait a moment . . .
(to the statue)
My master asks your lordship —
i' faith, not I, sir —
to sup with him.
Oh! oh! this is too dreadful! . . .
(The statue nods)
O Heaven! he nodded his head!

GIOVANNI
Va là, che se' un buffone.

LEPORELLO
Guardate ancor . . . padrone . . .

GIOVANNI
E che degg'io guardar?

LEPORELLO
Colla marmorea testa
ei fa . . . così . . . così . . .
(imita la statua)

GIOVANNI
(tra sé)
Colla marmorea testa
ei fa così . . . così!
(verso la statua)
Parlate, se potete:
verrete a cena?

COMMENDATORE
Sì.

LEPORELLO
Mover . . . mi . . . posso appena . . .
Mi manca, oh Dei! . . . la lena . . .
Per carità . . . partiamo . . .
Andiamo via di qua.

GIOVANNI
Bizzarra è inver la scena!
Verrà il buon vecchio a cena!
A prepararla andiamo:
partiamo via di qua.
(partono)

SCENA TREDICESIMA

Camera tetra in casa di Donna Anna.
Don Ottavio e Donna Anna.

RECITATIVO

OTTAVIO
Calmatevi, idol mio; di quel
ribaldo vedrem puniti in breve
i gravi eccessi: vendicati sarem.

GIOVANNI
What nonsense! You're a fool!

LEPORELLO
But look yourself, sir . . .

GIOVANNI
What is there to look at?

LEPORELLO
With his marble head
he nodded like this . . .
(imitating the statue)

GIOVANNI
(aside)
With his marble head
he nodded like this . . . !
(to the statue)
Speak then, if you can:
will you come to supper?

COMMENDATORE
Yes.

LEPORELLO
I can barely move for terror,
my heart fails me . . .
For God's sake, come on, sir:
let's be off from here.

GIOVANNI
A strange adventure this!
The greybeard will come to supper!
Let's go and prepare it:
we'll be off from here.
(exeunt)

SCENE 13

A darkened room in Donna Anna's
house. Don Ottavio and Donna Anna

RECITATIVE

OTTAVIO
Be calm, my dearest love: soon we'll see
the criminal's vile deeds punished,
and we shall be avenged.

92

ANNA
Ma il padre, oh Dio!

OTTAVIO
Convien chinare il ciglio
al volere del ciel. Respira, o cara!
Di tua perdita amara
fia domani, se vuoi, dolce compenso
questo cor, questa mano,
che il mio tenero amor . . .

ANNA
Oh Dei! che dite!
in sì tristi momenti . . .

OTTAVIO
E che! vorresti,
con indugi novelli,
accrescer le mie pene? Crudele!

23.   RECITATIVO ED ARIA

ANNA
Crudele? Ah no! mio bene!
troppo mi spiace allontanarti un
ben che lungamente la nostr'alma
desìa. Ma il mondo, oh Dio!
Non sedur la costanza
del sensibil mio core:
abbastanza per te mi parla amore.

ARIA

ANNA
Non mi dir, bell'idol mio,
che son io crudel con te:
tu ben sai quant'io t'amai,
tu conosci la mia fe'.
Calma, calma il tuo tormento,
se di duol non vuoi ch'io mora;
forse un giorno il cielo ancora
sentirà pietà di me.

(parte)

RECITATIVO

OTTAVIO
Ah, si segua il suo passo;
io vo' con lei dividere i martiri.

ANNA
But my father . . . O Heavens!

OTTAVIO
We must bow our heads
to the will of Providence. Look up,
beloved! For your bitter loss this heart,
this hand tomorrow shall make
fond recompense, if you will:
for my tender love . . .

ANNA
Alas! What say you
in this moment of sorrow?

OTTAVIO
Then would you increase
my longings by fresh delays?
Cruel one!

23.   RECITATIVE AND ARIA

ANNA
I cruel? Ah no, my dearest!
It grieves me much to postpone
a bliss we have for long desired . . .
But what would the world say?
Do not tempt the fortitude
of my tender heart,
which already pleads your loving cause.

ARIA

ANNA
Say not, my beloved,
that I am cruel to you:
you must know how much I loved you,
and you know that I am true.
Calm your torments,
if you would not have me die of grief:
one day, perhaps,
Heaven will smile again on me.

(exit)

RECITATIVE

OTTAVIO
Ah, I will follow her;
I will share her sorrows:

Saran meco men gravi i suoi sospiri.

(parte)

her grief then will be easier to bear.

(exit)

SCENA QUATTORDICESIMA

*Sala in casa di Don Giovanni, con
una mensa preparata. Don Giovanni
e Leporello. Servi alcuni Suonatori*

SCENE 14

*A hall in Don Giovanni's house, with
a table laid. Don Giovanni and Leporello,
servants and some musicians*

24. FINALE

GIOVANNI
Già la mensa è preparata:
(ai suonatori)
voi suonate, amici cari;
giacché spendo i miei danari
io mi voglio divertir.
(siede a mensa)
Leporello, presto in tavola.

LEPORELLO
Son prontissimo a servir.
(I suonatori cominciano)
Bravi! » Cosa rara. «
*(alludendo ad un pezzo di musica
nell'opera » La cosa rara «)*

GIOVANNI
Che ti par del bel concerto?

LEPORELLO
É conforme al vostro merto.

GIOVANNI
(mangiando)
Ah, che piatto saporito!

LEPORELLO
(a parte)
Ah, che barbaro appetito!
Che bocconi da gigante!
Mi par proprio di svenir.

GIOVANNI
(tra sé)
Nel veder i miei bocconi
gli par proprio di svenir.
(forte)
Piatto.

24. FINALE

GIOVANNI
Well, the table's ready.
(to the musicians)
Strike up, good friends;
since I'm spending money
let's have some entertainment.
(he sits at table)
Leporello, serve the supper!

LEPORELLO
At once, my lord . . .
(The musicians strike up)
Oh good! That's "Cosa rara".
*(referring to the opera
of that name)*

GIOVANNI
How do you like this music?

LEPORELLO
It's just the thing for you, sir.

GIOVANNI
(eating)
This is a tasty dish!

LEPORELLO
(aside)
What a ravenous appetite!
What enormous mouthfuls!
And I'm faint with hunger!

GIOVANNI
(aside)
While he watches me eat,
he is faint with hunger!
(aloud)
Take it away!

94

LEPORELLO
Servo.
(I suonatori cangiano la musica)

LEPORELLO
Evvivano »I litiganti «
*(alludendo ad altr'opera di
questo titolo)*

GIOVANNI
Versa il vino.
Eccellente marzimino!

LEPORELLO
(mangiando e brevendo di nascosto)
Questo pezzo di fagiano
piano, piano vo' inghiottir.

GIOVANNI
(tra sé)
Sta mangiando quel marrano;
fingero di non capir.

LEPORELLO
*(ai suonatori che di nuovo
cangiano motivo)*
Questa poi purtroppo la conosco.

GIOVANNI
(senza guardarlo)
Leporello!

LEPORELLO
(col boccone in gola)
Padron mio.

GIOVANNI
Parla schietto, mascalzone.

LEPORELLO
Non mi lascia una flussione
le parole proferir.

GIOVANNI
Mentre io mangio fischia un poco.

LEPORELLO
Non so far.

GIOVANNI
Cos'è?

LEPORELLO
Yes, sir!
(The musicians change the tune)

LEPORELLO
Hurrah for "I litiganti"
*(referring to the opera of
that name)*

GIOVANNI
Pour the wine.
This is a good vintage!

LEPORELLO
(secretly eating and drinking)
Very, very quietly
I'll swallow this bit of pheasant.

GIOVANNI
(aside)
The rascal's eating;
I'll pretend not to notice.

LEPORELLO
*(to the musicians, who have changed
their tune again)*
Now that tune I know only too well.

GIOVANNI
(not looking at him)
Leporello!

LEPORELLO
(with his mouth full)
Coming, sir.

GIOVANNI
Speak clearly, rascal.

LEPORELLO
I've something in my throat
that prevents me, sir.

GIOVANNI
Whistle the tune while I'm eating.

LEPORELLO
I can't, sir.

GIOVANNI
And why not, pray?

LEPORELLO
Scusate. Sì eccellente è il vostro
cuoco che lo volli anch'io provar.

GIOVANNI
(tra sé)
Sì eccellente è il cuoco mio
che lo volle anch'ei provar.

SCENA QUINDICESIMA

Donna Elvira e detti

ELVIRA
(entrando disperata)
L'ultima prova
dell'amor mio
ancor vogl'io
fare con te.
Più non rammento
gl'inganni tuoi;
pietade io sento . . .

GIOVANNI E LEPORELLO
Cos'è, cos'è?

*(Don Giovanni si alza in piedi,
e assoglie Donna Elvira ridendo)*

ELVIRA
(s'inginocchia)
Da te non chiede
quest'alma oppressa
della sua fede
qualche merce'.

GIOVANNI
Mi meraviglio!
Cosa volete?
(per beffarla s'inginocchia)
Se non sorgete
non resto in pie'.

ELVIRA
Ah, non deridere gli affanni miei.

LEPORELLO
(tra sé)
Quasi da piangere mi fa costei.

LEPORELLO
Forgive me! Your cook is such a paragon
that I thought I'd try him too.

GIOVANNI
(aside)
My cook is such a paragon
he thought he'd try him too!

SCENE 15

Donna Elvira and the above

ELVIRA
(enters distractedly)
Let me
give you
one last proof
of my love.
I'll reproach you no more
for your deception:
I come to save you . . .

GIOVANNI E LEPORELLO
What's this? what's this?

*(Don Giovanni rises and welcomes
Donna Elvira laughing)*

ELVIRA
(kneeling)
My heavy,
faithful heart
seeks no pity
from you.

GIOVANNI
I'm astonished!
What do you want then?
(in mockery kneels beside her)
If you won't get up,
I must kneel too.

ELVIRA
Ah, do not mock me in my anguish.

LEPORELLO
(aside)
She has me almost in tears.

96

GIOVANNI _alzandosi e facendo alzare_ _Donna Elvira)_ o te deridere! Cielo! e perché? _con affettata tenerezza)_ Che vuoi, mio bene?	GIOVANNI _(getting up and assisting Donna Elvira_ _to rise)_ I mock you? But why? _(with affected tenderness)_ What are you asking, dearest?
ELVIRA Che vita cangi.	ELVIRA That you should change your way of living.
GIOVANNI Brava!	GIOVANNI Fine words!
ELVIRA Cor perfido!	ELVIRA Heartless man!
GIOVANNI Lascia ch'io mangi; E, se ti piace, mangia con me.	GIOVANNI Do let me eat: you can join me if you wish.
ELVIRA Rèstati, barbaro! nel lezzo immondo, esempio orribile d'iniquità.	ELVIRA Monster! Then remain a horrible example in the stinking pit of your iniquity.
parte)	_(exit)_
LEPORELLO _tra sé)_ Se non si muove al suo dolore, di sasso ha il core, o cor non ha.	LEPORELLO _(aside)_ If he's not moved by her grief, he has a heart of stone or no heart at all.
GIOVANNI Vivan le femmine! Viva il buon vino! Sostegno e gloria d'umanità!	GIOVANNI Here's to women and good wine, the support and glory of mankind!
ELVIRA Ah!	ELVIRA Ah!
di dentro: poi rientra, mettendo _un grido orribile, traversa la scena_ _fuggendo, esce da un'altra parte._ _I suonatori partono)_	_(from within: then returns, with a terrible_ _scream, rushing across the stage and_ _out the other side._ _The musicians leave)_
GIOVANNI E LEPORELLO Che grido è questo mai?	GIOVANNI AND LEPORELLO What is she screaming for?

GIOVANNI
Va a veder che cos'è stato.

GIOVANNI
Go and see what's the matter.

LEPORELLO
(esce e, prima di tornare, mette
un grido ancor più forte)

LEPORELLO
(goes out and, before returning, utters
an even more terrible cry)

GIOVANNI
Che grido indiavolato!
Leporello, che cos'è?

GIOVANNI
What a fiendish cry!
Leporello, what is it?

LEPORELLO
(entra spaventato e chiude l'uscio)
Ah! signor . . . per carità . . .
Non andate fuor di qua . . .
L'uom di sasso . . . l'uomo bianco . . .
Ah, padron . . . io gelo . . . io manco . . .
Se vedeste che figura . . .
Se sentiste come fa . . .
Ta ta ta ta ta ta ta.

LEPORELLO
(returns in terror, locking the door)
Oh my lord! . . . for mercy's sake . . .
don't go out that door! . . .
The stone statue, all white . . .
Oh master, I'm scared to death . . .
If you but saw his face . . .
if you but heard his steps go . . .
tramp, tramp, tramp, tramp!

GIOVANNI
Non capisco niente affatto:
tu sei matto in verità.

GIOVANNI
I don't understand a word you say:
you must be out of your mind.

(Si batte alla porta)

(There is knocking at the door)

LEPORELLO
Ah! sentite!

LEPORELLO
Oh listen!

GIOVANNI
Qualcun batte.
Apri.

GIOVANNI
Someone's knocking.
Open!

LEPORELLO
Io tremo . . .

LEPORELLO
I dare not . . .

GIOVANNI
Apri, ti dico.

GIOVANNI
Open, I say!

LEPORELLO
No! Ah!

LEPORELLO
No! Ah!

GIOVANNI
Per togliermi d'intrico
ad aprir io stesso andrò.

GIOVANNI
To clear up this nonsense
I'll open the door myself.

(Prende il lume e la spada sguainata
e va ad aprire)

(Takes the lamp and a drawn sword and
goes to open the door)

LEPORELLO
(tra sé)
Non vo' più veder l'amico;
pian pianin m'asconderò.

(si cela sotto la tavola)

SCENA SEDICESIMA

Il Commendatore e detti

COMMENDATORE
Don Giovanni, a cenar teco
m'invitasti, e son venuto.

GIOVANNI
Non l'avrei giammai creduto:
ma farò quel che potrò.
Leporello, un'altra cena.
fa che subito si porti.

LEPORELLO
*(facendo capolino di sotto
alla tavola)*
Ah! padron . . . siam tutti morti . . .

GIOVANNI
(tirandolo fuori)
Vanne, dico.

COMMENDATORE
(a Leporello, che è in atto di partire)
Ferma un po'.
Non si pasce di cibo mortale
chi si pasce di cibo celeste;
altre cure più gravi di queste,
altra brama quaggiù mi guido.

LEPORELLO
(tra sé)
La terzana d'avere mi sembra . . .
E le membra fermar più non so.

GIOVANNI
Parla dunque: che chiedi?
che vuoi?

COMMENDATORE
Parlo, ascolta: più tempo non ho.

LEPORELLO
(aside)
I've no wish to see any more, believe me;
I'll hide myself away.

(hides under the table)

SCENE 16

The Commendatore and the above

COMMENDATORE
Don Giovanni, you invited me
to sup with you: I have come.

GIOVANNI
I would never have believed it;
but I'll do the best I can.
Leporello, have another supper
laid at once.

LEPORELLO
*(peeping out from under
the table)*
Oh my lord . . . we are all dead men . . .

GIOVANNI
(pulling him out)
Go, I tell you.

COMMENDATORE
(to Leporello, as he is going)
No, stay!
He who has eaten the food of heaven
has no need of mortal food.
A graver purpose than this,
another mission has brought me hither.

LEPORELLO
(aside)
It's as if I had the ague:
I cannot keep from shaking.

GIOVANNI
Pray tell me, what do you seek then?
What is it?

COMMENDATORE
Hear what I say: my time is short.

GIOVANNI
Parla, parla: ascoltando ti sto.

COMMENDATORE
Tu m'invitasti a cena:
il tuo dovere or sai.
Rispondimi: verrai
tu a cenar meco?

LEPORELLO
Oibò! Tempo non ha . . .
scusate. .

GIOVANNI
A torto di viltate tacciato mai sarò.

COMMENDATORE
Risolvi.

GIOVANNI
Ho già risolto.

COMMENDATORE
Verrai?

LEPORELLO
(a Don Giovanni)
Dite di no.

GIOVANNI
Ho fermo il core in petto:
non ho timor, verrò.

COMMENDATORE
Dammi la mano in pegno.

GIOVANNI
(porgendogli la mano)
Eccola . . . Ohimé! . . .

COMMENDATORE
Cos'hai?

GIOVANNI
Che gelo è questo mai!

COMMENDATORE
Pèntiti, cangia vita:
è l'ultimo momento.

GIOVANNI
Speak then: I am listening.

COMMENDATORE
To supper you invited me.
You know a host's obligation:
so answer, will you in turn
come and sup with me?

LEPORELLO
For God's sake, no!
He's not free: excuse him!

GIOVANNI
Never will I be accused of cowardice.

COMMENDATORE
Make your decision.

GIOVANNI
I am decided.

COMMENDATORE
You'll come?

LEPORELLO
(to Don Giovanni)
Tell him no!

GIOVANNI
My heart is firm within me.
I know no fear: I'll come.

COMMENDATORE
Give me your hand in token!

GIOVANNI
(offering his hand)
Here it is . . . O God! . . .

COMMENDATORE
What is it?

GIOVANNI
It's colder than the tomb.

COMMENDATORE
Repent your sins:
your hour of doom is near.

GIOVANNI
(vuole sciogliersi, ma invano)
Non, no, ch'io non mi pento;
vanne lontan da me.

COMMENDATORE
Pèntiti, o scellerato.

GIOVANNI
No, vecchio infatuato.

COMMENDATORE
Pèntiti.

GIOVANNI
No.

COMMENDATORE E LEPORELLO
Sì.

GIOVANNI
No.

COMMENDATORE
Ah! tempo più non v'è.

*(Fuoco da diverse parti, il
Commendatore sparisce, e
s'apre una voragine.)*

GIOVANNI
Da qual tremore insolito . . .
Sento . . . assalir . . . gli spiriti . . .
Donde escono que' vortici
di foco pien d'orror?

CORO
Tutto a tue colpe è poco:
vieni, c'è un mal peggior.

GIOVANNI
Chi l'anima mi lacera!
Chi m'agita le viscere!
Che strazio! ohimè! che smania!
Che inferno! che terror!

LEPORELLO
(tra sé)
Che ceffo disperato!
Che gesti d'un dannato!
Che gridi! che lamenti!

GIOVANNI
(vainly trying to free himself)
For me there's no repentance.
Avaunt! away from me!

COMMENDATORE
Repent, wicked man!

GIOVANNI
No, you old dotard!

COMMENDATORE
Repent!

GIOVANNI
No.

COMMENDATORE AND LEPORELLO
Yes!

GIOVANNI
No!

COMMENDATORE
Your time has come!

*(Flames spring up all round. The
Commendatore disappears and a
chasm opens.)*

GIOVANNI
Every limb is seized
with a trembling I have never known . . .
Whence come these hideous
spurts of flame?

CHORUS
No doom is too great for your sins!
Worse torments await you below!

GIOVANNI
My soul is torn in agony,
my body is in torture!
Ah! what torment, what madness!
The terrors of Hell . . .

LEPORELLO
(aside)
Doom is in his face,
and damnation in his gestures!
What shrieks! what cries!

101

Come mi fa terror!

I am dead with fright!

CORO
Tutto a tue colpe è poco:
vieni; c'è un mal peggior.

CHORUS
No doom is too great for your sins!
Worse torments await you below!

*(Cresce il fuoco, compariscono
diverse furie, s'impossessano di
Don Giovanni, e seco lui sprofondano)*

*(The flames increase. Furies spring
up, seize Don Giovanni and sink
into the earth with him)*

SCENA ULTIMA

FINALE

*Leporello, Donna Elvira, Donna
Anna, Zerlina, Don Ottavio,
Masetto con ministri di giustizia*

*Leporello, Donna Elvira, Donna
Anna, Zerlina, Don Ottavio,
Masetto with ministers of justice.*

TUTTI
(meno Leporello)
Ah! dov'è il perfido?
Dov'è l'indegno?
Tutto il mio sdegno
sfogar io vo'.

ALL
(except Leporello)
Where is the miscreant?
Where is the criminal?
Now shall our retribution
be unleashed.

ANNA
Solo mirandolo
stretto in catene
alle mie pene calma darò.

ANNA
Only seeing him
bound in chains will calm
my torments.

LEPORELLO
Più non sperate
di ritrovarlo . . .
Più non cercate . . .
Lontano andò.

LEPORELLO
Do not hope
ever to find him again . . .
No need to search . . .
he's far away now.

TUTTI
Cos'è? favella
Via, presto, sbrigati!

TUTTI
But what has happened?
Quick, tell us!

LEPORELLO
Venne un colosso . . .
Ma se non posso . . .
Tra fumo e foco . . .
Badate un poco . . .
L'uomo di sasso . . .
Fermate il passo . . .
Giusto là sotto . . .
Diede il gran botto . . .
Giusto là il diavolo
sel trangugiò.

LEPORELLO
There came a statue . . .
how can I say it? . . .
through smoke and flame . . .
look around you!
The man of marble . . .
Heaven defend us! . . .
put his great foot
down just there . . .
and just there
the devil dragged him down.

TUTTI	ALL
Stelle! che sento!	What story is this?
LEPORELLO	LEPORELLO
Vero è l'evento.	Every word of it's true.
TUTTI	ALL
Ah, certo è l'ombra	That must have been the spectre
che s'incontrò.	that was seen.
OTTAVIO	OTTAVIO
Or che tutti, o mio tesoro,	Now, my dearest, that heaven
vendicati siam dal cielo,	has avenged us all,
porgi, porgi a me un ristoro,	grant me, I beg, my reward:
non mi far languire ancor.	do not leave me still to languish.
ANNA	ANNA
Lascia, o caro, un anno ancora	Give me but a year
allo sfogo del mio cor.	for my heart to heal.
Al desìo di ch t' adora	A beloved's plea
ceder deve un fido amor.	is a command.
OTTAVIO	OTTAVIO
Al desìo di chi m'adora	A beloved's plea
ceder deve un fido amor.	is a command.
ELVIRA	ELVIRA
Io men vado in un ritiro	I will enter a covent
a finir la vita mia!	there to end my life!
ZERLINA E MASETTO	ZERLINA AND MASETTO
Noi, Zerlina e Masetto,	We, Zerlina and Masetto,
a casa andiamo	we'll go home together
a cenare in compagnia.	and have our dinner.
LEPORELLO	LEPORELLO
Ed io vado all'osteria	And I'll go to the inn
a trovar padron miglior.	and find myself a better master.
ZERLINA, MASETTO E LEPORELLO	ZERLINA, MASETTO AND LEPORELLO
Resti dunque quel birbon	Let the scoundrel remain below
con Proserpina e Pluton;	with Proserpine and Pluto.
e noi tutti, o buona gente,	And we, good people,
ripetiam allegramente	will gaily sing the ancient
l'antichissima canzon:	moral:
TUTTI	ALL
Questo è il fin di chi fa mal!	This is the evil-doer's end!
E de' perfidi la morte	Sinners finally meet their just reward,
alla vita è sempre ugual.	and always will.

IDOMENEO

Libretto by Giambattista Varesco

DRAMATIS PERSONAE

IDOMENEO, *King of Crete*
IDAMANTE, *his son*
ELECTRA, *Greek princess, daughter of Agamemnon*
ILIA, *Trojan princess, daughter of Priam*
ARBACE, *Idomeneo's counsellor*
HIGH PRIEST
VOICE OF NEPTUNE

Chorus of Cretans, Trojan prisoners, etc

The opera is set in the Cretan port of Sidon, after the end of the Trojan War.

Synopsis

ACT I

A room in the royal palace. Ilia, royal survivor of the sack of Troy, bemoans her captive lot. A storm separated the returning ships, and she was rescued from the wreckage by Idamante, with whom she is now secretly in love. Idamante enters to announce that his father's ship has been sighted, and confesses that he loves Ilia. She reminds him of their differing status of prince/captive, Greek/Trojan. Idamante grants the Trojan prisoners their freedom. Arbace bears news of a sudden offshore storm that has destroyed Idomeneo's fleet. All hurry away save Electra, who has already voiced her disapproval of Idamante's clemency to the Trojans in general and Ilia in particular and now gives vent to her jealously possessive feelings for Idamante.

A rocky shore. Idomeneo is among the survivors of the storm. He recalls, and very much regrets, a rash vow made at the height of the tempest·to sacrifice to Neptune the first mortal he meets should he survive. A young man approaches— it is, of course, Idamante. When Idomeneo realises this, he rushes away in horror, much to his son's confusion and distress. The remainder of the survivors rejoice.

ACT II

The royal apartments. Idomeneo tells Arbace about his vow. Arbace suggests that if Idamante were out of the way, the god might be appeased by other means. Idomeneo resolves to send him to escort Electra home to Argos. From a conversation with Ilia, Idomeneo discerns her feelings for Idamante, and once more regrets his hasty vow. Electra thanks Idomeneo for his concern, and looks forward eagerly to being alone with Idamante.

The quay. While Idomeneo is seeing the royal travellers off, a storm arises and a fearful sea monster arises from the deep. The people ask what crime can have brought about this fresh scourge, and Idomeneo confesses that it is his, without going into detail. The people flee in terror.

ACT III

The palace gardens. Ilia sings of her secret love for Idamante. He enters to re-affirm his passion, and tells her that he is going to fight the monster, which continues to ravage the shores of Crete. Concern leads Ilia to reveal her love at last. Idomeneo and Electra enter. Idamante begs his father to explain his continuing hostility, but Idomeneo answers only with fresh orders to Idamante to leave Crete at once. Ilia offers in vain to accompany him, and Electra expresses her jealousy in a series of asides. Arbace reports the people's growing restlessness, and Idomeneo hurries away to calm them.

A square before the palace. The High Priest describes the horrors wrought by the monster, and demands that Idomeneo select a propitiary sacrifice. The king announces that it must be his own son, to the consternation of all.

Before the temple of Neptune. Preparations for the sacrifice are halted by the news that Idamante has slain the monster. He himself enters, dressed as a sacrificial victim, and begs Idomeneo strike the blow. Ilia urgently offers herself as an alternative (and equally willing) victim. The impasse is resolved by the disembodied voice of Neptune, who decrees that Idomeneo's vow will become null upon his abdication. Idamante is to be king, and Ilia his queen. Only Electra is disappointed by this outcome. The remainder call down the blessings of Cupid, Hymen and Juno upon the happy pair.

Atto primo

Act one

SCENA PRIMA

SCENE 1

Appartamenti d'Ilia nel palazzo
reale. Ilia sola

Ilia's apartments in the royal palace.
Ilia alone

RECITATIVO

RECITATIVE

ILIA
Quando avran fine omai l'aspre
sventure mie? Ilia infelice!
Di tempesta crudel misero avanzo,
del genitor, e de' germani priva,
del barbaro nemico misto col sangue
il sangue vittime generose,
a qual sorte più rea ti riserbano i
Numi? Pur vendicaste voi, di Priamo
e di Troja i danni e l'onte?
Perì la flotta Argiva, e Idomeneo
pasto forse sarà d'orca vorace . . .
Ma che mi giova, o ciel,
se al primo aspetto di quel prode
Idamante, che all'onde mi rapì,
l'odio deposi, e pria fù schiavo il
cor, che m'accorgessi d'essere
prigionera. Ah, qual contrasto, oh
Dio, d'opposti effetti mi destate
nel sen, odio ed amore!
Vendetta deggio a chi mi diè la vita,
gratitudine a chi vita mi rende . . .
O Ilia! O genitor, o prence, o sorte!
O vita sventurata, o dolce morte!
Ma che? M'ama Idamante?
Ah no; l'ingrato per Elettra sospira,
e quell' Elettra, meschina principessa,
esule d'Argo, d'Oreste alle sciagure
a queste arene fuggitiva, raminga,
e mia rivale. Quanti mi siete intorno,

ILIA
When will my bitter misfortunes
be ended? Unhappy Ilia,
wretched survivor of a dreadful tempest,
bereft of father and brothers,
the victims' blood spilt and mingled
with the blood of their savage foes,
for what harsher fate have the gods
preserved you? Are the loss and shame
of Priam and Troy avenged?
The Greek fleet is destroyed, and
Idomeneo perhaps will be a meal for hungry
fish . . . But what comfort is that to me, ye
heavens, if at the first sight of that valiant
Idamante who snatched me from the waves
I forgot my hatred, and my heart was
enslaved before I realised I was a
prisoner. Oh God, what a conflict
of warring emotions you rouse
in my breast, of hate and love!
I owe vengeance to him who gave me life,
gratitude to him who restored it . . .
O Ilia! O father, o prince, o destiny!
O ill-fated life, o sweet death!
But yet does Idamante love me?
Ah no; ungratefully he sighs for Electra;
and that Electra, unhappy princess,
an exile from Argos and the torments of
Orestes, who fled, a wanderer, to these
shores, is my rival. Ruthless

109

carnefici spietate? Orsù, sbranate
vendetta, gelosia, odio ed amore,
sbranate sì quest' infelice
core.

| butchers, how many of you surround
me? Then up and shatter vengeance,
jealousy, hate and love;
yes, shatter my unhappy heart.

1. ARIA

ILIA
Padre, germani, addio!
Vi foste, io vi perdei.
Grecia, cagion tu sei,
e un greco adorerò?
D'ingrata al sangue mio,
so che la colpa avrei;
ma quel sembiante, oh Dei,
odiare ancor non so.

1. ARIA

ILIA
Father, brothers, farewell!
You are no more; I have lost you.
Greece, you are the cause;
and shall I now love a Greek?
I know that I am guilty
of abandoning my kin;
but I cannot bring myself,
o gods, to hate that face.

RECITATIVO

Ecco Idamante, ahimè! Sen' vien.
Misero core, tu palpiti e paventi.
Deh cessate per poco, o miei
tormenti.

RECITATIVE

Alas, here is Idamante coming.
Unhappy heart, you flutter and falter.
O grant me some respite from my
torments.

SCENA SECONDA

Idamante con seguito, Ilia

IDAMANTE
(al seguito)
Radunate i Trojani, ite,
e la corte sia pronta
questo giorno a celebrar.

(I seguaci partono)

(ad Ilia)
Di dolce speme a un raggio
scema il mio duol.
Minerva della Grecia protettrice
involò al furor dell' onde il padre
mio; in mar, di qui non lunge,
comparser le sue navi;
indaga Arbace il sito, che a noi
toglie l'augusto aspetto.

SCENE 2

Idamante with his retinue, Ilia

IDAMANTE
(to his followers)
Go, assemble the Trojans,
and let the court prepare
the celebrate this day.

(Exeunt retinue)

(to Ilia)
My grief is diminished
by one ray of sweet hope.
Minerva, protectress of Greece,
saved my father from the waves' fury;
his ships have been sighted
at sea, not far from here;
Arbace is looking for the spot
where his noble face is kept from us.

ILIA
Non temer; difesa da Minerva è la
Grecia, e tutta ormai scoppiò sovra i
Trojan' l'ira de' Numi.

ILIA
Fear not: Greece is protected by Minerva,
while all the wrath of the gods
has burst upon the Trojans.

110

IDAMANTE
Del fato de' Trojani più non dolerti.
Sarà il figlio per lor quanto sarebbe
il genitor, e ogni altro vincitor
generoso. Ecco: abbian fine,
principessa, i lor guai; rendo lor
libertade, e omai fra noi sol
prigionero fia, sol fia, chi porta che
tua beltà legò care ritorte.

ILIA
Signor, che ascolto? Non saziaro
ancora d'implacabili Dei l'odio, lo
sdegno d'Ilion, le gloriose or
diroccate mura, ah, non più mura,
ma vasto e piano suol?
A eterno pianto dannate
son le nostre egre pupille?

IDAMANTE
Venere noi puni, di noi trionfa.
Quanto il mio genitor, ahi
rimembranza, soffri de' flutti in sen!
Agamemnòne vittima in Argo al fin,
a caro prezzo comprò que' suoi
trofei, e non contenta di tante stragi
ancor la Dea nemica, che fè?
Il mio cor trafisse, Ilia, co' tuoi bei
lumi più possenti de' suoi,
e in me vendica adesso i danni tuoi.

ILIA
Che dici?

IDAMANTE
Si, di Citerea il figlio
incogniti tormenti stillommi in petto;
a te pianto e scompiglio Marte portò,
cercò vendetta Amore in me de' mali
tuoi, quei vaghi rai, quei tuoi vezzi
adoprò. Ma all' amor mio d'ira e
rossor tu avvampi?

ILIA
In questi accenti mal soffro
un temerario ardir.
Deh pensa, Idamante, oh Dio,
il padre tuo qual' è, qual' era il mio.

IDAMANTE
Grieve no more over the Trojans' fate.
The son will treat them as the father,
or any other generous victor, would have
done. See, princess, their woes are ended:
I give them back their freedom,
and now one prisoner alone remains
among us, he who wears the sweet chains
in which your beauty binds him.

ILIA
What do I hear, my lord? Are the
hatred and scorn of the implacable gods
for Ilium not yet satisfied, now that its
glorious walls are destroyed — ah, no
longer walls but a vast and level plain?
Are our sad eyes condemned
to eternal weeping?

IDAMANTE
Venus punished us and triumphs over us.
How my father — alas the thought! —
suffered at heart in the waves!
Agamemnon, finally a victim in Argos,
bought his victory dear,
and the hostile goddess, still not content
with such massacre, what did she do?
She pierced my heart, Ilia, with your
lovely eyes, more potent than her own,
and now avenges your sufferings in me.

ILIA
What say you?

IDAMANTE
Yes, Cytherea's son has planted
unknown torments in my heart;
to you Mars has brought tears and
agitation, and Love, seeking revenge on
me for your wrongs, employed your
lovely eyes and your beauty. But you
turn red and flare up in anger at my love?

ILIA
I take ill the bold ardour
of these words.
Oh God! Consider, Idamante,
who your father is, and who mine was.

111

2. ARIA

IDAMANTE
Non ho colpa, e mi condanni,
idol mio, perche t'adoro.
Colpa è vostra, o Dei tiranni,
e di pena afflitto io moro
d'un error che mio non è.
Se tu il brami, al tuo impero
aprirommi questo seno;
ne' tuoi lumi il leggo, è vero,
ma me'l dica il labro almeno,
e non chiedo altra mercè.

RECITATIVO

ILIA
(vedendo condurre i prigionieri)
Ecco il misero resto de' Trojani,
dal nemico furor salvi.

IDAMANTE
Or quei ceppi io romperò,
vuò consolarli adesso.
(Ahi! Perchè tanto far non so a me
stesso!)

SCENA TERZA

*Trojani prigionieri, uomini e donne
Cretesi, e detti*

IDAMANTE
Scingete le catene, ed oggi il mondo,
o fedele Sidon suddita nostra,
vegga due gloriosi popoli
in dolce nodo avvinti,
a stretti di perfetta amistà.
Elena armò la Grecia e l'Asia,
ed ora disarma e riunisce ed Asia
e Grecia eroina novella,
principessa più amabile e più bella.

3. CORO DE' TROJANI E CRETESI

CORO
Godiam la pace, trionfi Amore,
ora ogni core giubilerà.

2. ARIA

IDAMANTE
The fault is not mine, and you condemn
me, my love, because I adore you.
The fault is yours, tyrannical gods,
and I die of distress and pain
for a crime which is not mine.
If you so desire it, at your command
I will pierce this breast of mine;
I read it in your eyes, it's true,
but at least tell me with your lips,
and I will ask no other mercy.

RECITATIVE

ILIA
(watching the prisoners led in)
Behold the wretched remnant of the
Trojans, saved from the enemy's fury.

IDAMANTE
Now I will break their bonds
and give them consolation.
(Why cannot I do as much for
myself!)

SCENE 3

*Trojan prisoners, Cretan men and women,
and the above*

IDAMANTE
Loosen their fetters, and today the world,
o faithful subjects of Sidon,
shall see two glorious peoples
united in the knot of friendship,
bound together in perfect harmony.
Helen armed Greece and Asia,
but now a new heroine disarms
and reunites Asia and Greece,
a princess more kindly and more lovely.

3. CHORUS OF TROJANS AND CRETANS

CHORUS
Let us enjoy peace, let Love triumph;
now every heart will rejoice.

DUE CRETESI	TWO CRETAN GIRLS
Grazie a chi estinse faci di guerra;	Thanks to him who extinguished the
or si la terra riposo avrà.	torches of war: now the land can have peace.

DUE TROJANI	TWO TROJANS
A voi dobbiamo, pietosi Numi,	We owe our liberty to you, merciful gods,
e a quei bei lumi la libertà.	and to those lovely eyes.

SCENA QUARTA   SCENE 4

Elettra, agitata di gelosia, e detti   *Electra, in jealous excitement, and the above*

RECITATIVO   RECITATIVE

ELETTRA	ELECTRA
Prence, signor, tutta la Grecia	My lord prince, you offend the whole of
oltraggi, tu proteggi il nemico.	Greece by protecting the enemy.

IDAMANTE	IDAMANTE
Veder basti alla Grecia vinto il	Let it suffice Greece to have seen her
nemico. Opra di me più degna a	enemy vanquished. Prepare yourself, o
mirar s'apparecchi, o principessa;	princess, to see a deed more worthy of me,
vegga il vinto felice.	to behold the vanquished happy.
Arbace viene . . .	Arbace approaches . . .
ma qual pianto ch'annunzia?	but what do these laments forebode?

SCENA QUINTA   SCENE 5

Arbace e detti   *Arbace, the above*

ARBACE	ARBACE
Mio signore, de' mali più terribil . . .	My lord, most terrible news . . .

IDAMANTE	IDAMANTE
Più non vive il genitor?	Is my father no longer alive?

ARBACE	ARBACE
Non vive! Quel che Marte far non	No longer! What Mars could not do till
potè fin or, fece Nettuno, l'inesorabil	now Neptune, that inexorable god, has
Nume; e degl' eroi il più degno, ora	done; and the noblest of heroes, I now
il riseppi, presso a straniera sponda	learn, was drowned, near a foreign
affogato mori!	shore!

IDAMANTE	IDAMANTE
Ilia, de' viventi eccoti il più meschin!	Ilia, I am the unhappiest of mortals!
Or si dal cielo soddisfatta sarai . . .	Now indeed Heaven will have satisfied
barbaro fato! Corrasi al lido!	you! Cruel fate! Let us hurry to the shore!
Ahimè! Son disperato.	Alas, I am in despair.
(partono Arbace ed Idamante)	*(Exeunt Arbace and Idamante)*

113

ILIA

Dell' Asia i danni ancora troppo
risento, e pur d'un grand' eroe al
nome, al caso, il cor parmi
commosso, e negargli i sospir,
ah no, non posso.
(parte)

SCENA SESTA

Elettra sola

ELETTRA

Estinto è Idomeneo?
Tutto a miei danni, tutto congiura il
ciel! Può a suo talento Idamante
disporre d'un impero, e del cor;
e a me non resta ombra di speme?
O mio dispetto, ahi lassa! Vedrò,
vedrà la Grecia, a suo gran scorno,
una schiava Trojana di quel soglio,
e del talamo a parte . . .
Invano Elettra ami l'ingrato . . .
e soffre una figlia d'un rè, ch'ha rè
vassalli, ch'una vil schiava aspiri al
grand'acquisto? O sdegno! O smanie!
O duol! Più non resisto!

4. ARIA

ELETTRA

Tutte nel cor vi sento,
furie del crudo averno,
lunge a si gran tormento
amor, mercè, pietà.
Chi mi rubò quel core,
quel che tradito ha il mio,
provin' dal mio furore,
vendetta e crudeltà.

SCENA SETTIMA

*Spiagge del mare agitato. Rottami
di navi sul lido.*

5. CORO

Pietà! Numi pietà!
Ajuto, o giusti Numi!
A noi volgete il lumi!
Il ciel, il mare, il vento

ILIA

I still feel all too keenly Asia's wrongs,
and yet at the name, at the
fate of a great hero my heart must be
moved, and I cannot deny him my tears.
(exit)

SCENE 6

Electra alone

ELECTRA

Is Idomeneo dead? Heaven conspires
to cross me in everything.
Idamante can, at his will,
dispose of an empire and of his heart;
and shall no shadow of hope remain for
me? Unfortunate and unhappy that I am,
I shall see, and Greece will see,
to its shame, a Trojan slave
share the throne and the bridal bed . . .
In vain, Electra, you love this ingrate . . .
Shall the daughter of a king, who has
kings as vassals, suffer a lowly slave to
aspire to these great honours? Shame!
Fury! Grief! I can bear it no more!

4. ARIA

ELECTRA

In my heart I feel you all,
Furies of bitter Hades;
far from such fierce torment
be love, pity or mercy.
Let her who stole that heart
which betrayed mine
feel my fury
and cruel revenge.

SCENE 7

*The sea-coast, with an angry sea. Ships'
wreckage on the shore.*

5. CHORUS

Ye Gods, have mercy!
Help, o just gods!
Turn your gaze on us.
The sky, the sea, the wind

114

opprimon di spavento.
braccio a cruda morte
spinge l'empia sorte!
artono)

oppress us with fear.
Pitiless fate thrusts us
into the arms of dreadful death!
(exeunt)

ENA OTTAVA

omeneo con seguito

CITATIVO

SCENE 8

Idomeneo with his followers

RECITATIVE

OMENEO
co ci salvi alfin.
voi, di Marte e di Nettuno all'ire,
e vittorie, ai stenti, fidi seguaci
ei, lasciatemi per poco qui solo
pirar, e al ciel natio confidar
passato affanno mio.
seguaci partono)
anquillo è il mar,
ra soave spira di dolce calma,
e cerulee sponde il biondo Dio
dora; ovunque io miro,
tto di pace in sen riposa e gode.
sol su queste aride spiagge
affanno e da disagio estenuato,
ella calma, o Nettuno, in me non
ovo, che al tuo regno impetrai.
mezzo a flutti e scogli,
ll'ira tua sedotto,
e lo scampo dal naufragio chiedei,
n olocausto, il primo de' mortali,
e qui intorno infelice s'aggiri,
'are tue pien di terror promisi.
' empio voto eccomi in salvo si,
a non in pace.
a son pur quelle, o Dio, le care
ura, dove la prima io trassi aura
ale? Lungi da si gran tempo, ah,
n qual core ora vi rivedrò,
appena in seno da voi accolto,
misero innocente, dovrò svenar!
voto insano, atroce! Giuramento
udel! Ah qual de' Numi mi serba
cor in vita; O qual di voi mi porge
nen aita?

IDOMENEO
We are here, safe at last.
O you who, braving the wrath of Mars and
Neptune, followed me loyally in victory
and hardship, leave me here alone a while
to breathe, and to confide to my
native sky the anguish I have suffered.
(Exeunt followers)
The ocean is calm,
the sweet breeze blows gently,
and the young god gilds the shores of the
sea; wherever I look,
everything rests in peace and joy.
Only I, o Neptune, prostrated by suffering
and hardship on these arid shores,
do not feel within me that calm
I attained in your kingdom.
Amidst waves and rocks,
cowering at your wrath, I appealed
to you for rescue from shipwreck,
and in terror promised to sacrifice
to your altar the first unfortunate mortal
who should come by.
By that impious vow here I am,
indeed safe, but not at peace.
But are those truly, o God, the dear walls
within which I drew my first breath of
life? Away for so long, ah, with what a
heavy heart I now see you again
if, scarcely received into your bosom,
I must condemn to death a wretched
innocent! O insane, hateful vow! Cruel
oath! Ah, which of the gods preserves my
life? Which of you will
help me?

ARIA

OMENEO
drommi intorno

6. ARIA

IDOMENEO
I shall see about me

l'ombra dolente,
che notte e giorno,
sono innocente,
m'accennerà.
Nel sen trafitto,
nel corpo esangue
il mio delitto
lo sparso sangue
m'additerà.
Qual spavento,
qual dolore!
Di tormento
questo core
quante volte morirà!

a lamenting shade
which night and day
will cry to me
"I am innocent".
The blood spilt
from his pierced breast,
his pale corpse
will point out to me
my crime.
What horror,
what grief!
How many times
this heart
will die of torment!

RECITATIVO

IDOMENEO
Cieli! Che veggo!
Ecco la sventurata vittima, ahime,
s'appressa . . . Oh qual dolore mostra
quel ciglio! Mi si gela il sangue,
fremo d'orror, e vi fia grata, o Numi,
leggitima vi sembra ostia umana
innocente? E queste mani le
ministre saran? Mani esecrande!
Barbari, ingiusti Numi! Are nefande!

RECITATIVE

IDOMENEO
Heavens! What do I see? Here, alas
is the unfortunate victim
approaching . . . Oh what grief that face
shows! My blood freezes, I tremble with
horror; and does it please you, o gods,
and seem to you right to sacrifice an
innocent person? Must my hands be
the instruments? Accursed hands!
Savage, unjust gods! Detestable altars!

SCENA NONA

Idamante, Idomeneo

IDAMANTE
Spiagge romite e voi scoscese rupi,
testimoni al mio duol siate,
e cortesi di questo vostro albergo
a un agitato cor.
Quanto spiegate di mia sorte
il rigor solinghi orrori!
Vedo fra quelli avvanzi di fracassate
navi su quel lido sconosciuto
guerrier. Voglio ascoltarlo, vuò
confortarlo, e voglio in letizia
cangiar quel suo cordoglio.
Sgombra, o guerrier, qual tu ti sia il
timore; eccoti pronto a tuo
soccorso quello che in questo clima
offrir te'l può.

SCENE 9

Idamante, Idomeneo

IDAMANTE
Lonely shores, and you rugged cliffs,
bear witness to my sorrow
and in kindness give your shelter
to an agitated heart.
How your remote horror accords
with the harshness of my fate!
I see, amid the remnants of wrecked
ships, an unknown warrior on that
beach. I would hear him, comfort
him, and change his anguish to gladness.
Put aside your fear, o warrior,
whoever you are; here
ready to aid you is one
who in this land has power to do so.

IDOMENEO
(Più il guardo, più mi strugge il
dolor.) De' giorni miei il resto a te
dovrò; tu quale avrai premio da
me?

IDAMANTE
Premio al mio cor sarà l'esser pago
d'averti sollevato, difeso. Ahi
troppo, amico, dalle miserie mie
instrutto io fui a intenerirmi alle
miserie altrui.

IDOMENEO
(Qual voce, qual pietà;
il mio sen trafigge!)
Misero tu? Che dici?
Ti son conte le tue sventure appien?

IDAMANTE
Dell' amor mio, cielo, il più caro
oggetto, in quelli abissi spinto
giace l'eroe Idomeneo estinto;
ma tu sospiri e piangi? T'è noto
Idomeneo?

IDOMENEO
Uom più di questo deplorabil non
v'è, non v'è chi plachi il fato suo
austero.

IDAMANTE
Che favelli? Vive egli ancor?
(Oh Dei! Torno a sperar.)
Ah dimmi amico, dimmi, dov'è?
Dov'è qual dolce aspetto vita me
renderà?

IDOMENEO
Ma d'onde nasce questa, che per lui
nutri tenerezza d'amor?

IDAMANTE
Potessi almeno a lui stesso
gli affetti miei spiegare!

IDOMENEO
(Pur quel sembiante non m'è tutto
stranier; un non so che ravviso in
quel.)

IDOMENEO
(The more I look at him, the more I am
consumed with grief.) I will be indebted
to you for the rest of my days; what
reward would you have of me?

IDAMANTE
The reward in my heart will be the
satisfaction of having saved and protected
you. Ah, my friend, my own troubles
have taught me all too well to sympathise
with those of others.

IDOMENEO
(Such a voice, such compassion;
it pierces my heart!)
Are you unhappy? What are you saying?
Are your misfortunes really so many?

IDAMANTE
The dearest object of my love, o heavens,
the hero Idomeneo lies dead in these
depths. But you sigh and weep;
do you know
Idomeneo?

IDOMENEO
No man is more to be pitied than he;
none can alleviate his harsh
fate.

IDAMANTE
What are you saying? Is he still alive?
(Ye Gods, my hopes return.)
Ah tell me, my friend, say, where is he?
Where is that kind face which will
restore my life?

IDOMENEO
But whence comes it, that for him
you nurture such loving tenderness?

IDAMANTE
Could I but tell him in person
of my feelings?

IDOMENEO
(Yet this face is not entirely strange to
me; something about it is
familiar.)

IDAMANTE
(Pensoso il mesto sguardo in me egli
fissa; e pur a quella voce, a quel
ciglio, a quel gesto, uom mi
rassembra o in corte o in campo a
me noto, ed amico.)

IDOMENEO
Tu mediti?

IDAMANTE
Tu mi contempli e taci?

IDOMENEO
Perchè quel tuo parlar si mi
conturba?

IDAMANTE
E qual mi sento anch'io
turbamento nell'alma?
Ah, più non posso il pianto ritener.

IDOMENEO
Ma di, qual fonte sgorga quel pianto?
E quel si acerbo duol, che per
Idomeneo tanto ti affligge?

IDAMANTE
Ah, ch'egli è il padre.

IDOMENEO
(Oh Dio!)
Parla, di chi è il padre?

IDAMANTE
È il padre mio!

IDOMENEO
Spietatissimi Dei!

IDAMANTE
Meco compiangi del padre mio il
destin?

IDOMENEO
Ah figlio!

IDAMANTE
Ah padre! Ah Numi! Dove son io?
O qual trasporto! Soffri, genitor
adorato, che al tuo seno . . . e che un

IDAMANTE
(Pensively he fixes on me a mournful
look; yet with that voice, that face, that
manner, he resembles someone known to
to me as a friend, either at court or in
the field.)

IDOMENEO
You are lost in thought?

IDAMANTE
You gaze at me in silence?

IDOMENEO
Why does your voice so perturb
me?

IDAMANTE
And why do I too feel
such agitation in my heart?
Ah, I can no longer restrain my tears.

IDOMENEO
But tell me, from what fount spring those
tears? And what is the bitter grief,
that for Idomeneo you are so distressed?

IDAMANTE
Ah, because he is the father.

IDOMENEO
(Oh God!)
Speak, whose father is he?

IDAMANTE
He is my father!

IDOMENEO
Most cruel gods!

IDAMANTE
Do you mourn with me my father's
fate?

IDOMENEO
My son!

IDAMANTE
My father! O gods, where am I?
What delight! Beloved father, let me
come to your breast and embrace . . .

amplesso ... Ahimè! Perche ti sdegni?
Disperato mi fuggi? Ah dove?

Alas! Why do you spurn me?
You fly from me in despair — but where?

IDOMENEO
Non mi seguir, te'l vieto!
Meglio per te saria
il non avermi veduto or qui;
paventa il rivedermi!
(parte in fretta)

IDOMENEO
Do not follow me! I forbid it!
It would have been better for you
not to have seen me here;
beware of seeing me again!
(hurries away)

SCENA DECIMA

SCENE 10

Idamante solo

Idamante alone

IDAMANTE
Ah qual gelido orror m'ingombra i
sensi! Lo vedo appena, il riconosco,
e a miei teneri accenti
in un balen s'invola;
Misero! In che l'offesi,
e come mai quel sdegno io meritai,
quelle minaccie?
Vuò seguirlo e veder, o sorte dura,
qual mi sovrasti ancor più rea
sventura.

IDAMANTE
Ah, what icy horror numbs my senses!
Hardly do I see and recognise him
than, at my tender words,
he abruptly flees.
Alas! How did I offend him
and how have I deserved that anger
and those threats?
I will follow and see, harsh fate,
what more cruel misfortune yet awaits
me.

7. ARIA

7. ARIA

IDAMANTE
Il padre adorato
ritrovo, e lo perdo.
Mi fugge sdegnato,
fremendo d'orror.
Morire credei
di gioja e d'amore,
or, barbari Dei,
m'uccide il dolor.
(parte)

IDAMANTE
My beloved father
I find again, only to lose him.
He scorns and flies me,
trembling with horror.
I thought I would die
of joy and love,
but, cruel gods,
grief is killing me.
(exit)

SCENA UNDICESIMA

SCENE 11

8. MARCIA

8. MARCH

*Sbarcono le truppe Cretesi arrivate
con Idomeneo: le donne Cretesi
accorrono e sfogano la vicendevole
gioia con un ballo grande.*

*The Cretan troops who arrived with
Idomeneo disembark: Cretan women run
up, and all give vent to their mutual joy
in a dance.*

9. CORO
Nettuno s'onori!
Quel nome risuoni,

9. CHORUS
Let Neptune be honoured!
Let his name resound

119

quel Nume s'adori,
sovrano del mar.
Con danze e con suoni
convien festeggiar.
(Soli)
Da lunge ei mira
di Giove l'ira,
e in un baleno
và all'Eghe in seno,
da regal sede
tosto provede,
fa i generosi
destrier squammosi,
ratto acoppiar.
Dall' onde fuore
suonan sonore
tritoni araldi
robusti e baldi
buccine intorno.
Già riede il giorno,
che il gran tridente
il mar furente
seppe domar.
Su conca d'oro,
regio decoro,
spira Nettuno.
Scherza Portuno
ancor bambino
col suo delfino,
con Anfitrite;
or noi di Dite
fè trionfar.
Nereide amabili,
ninfe adorabili,
che alla gran Dea,
con Galatea
corteggio fate,
deh ringraziate
per noi quei Numi,
che i nostri lumi
fero asciugar.
(Tutti)
Or suonin le trombe,
solenne ecatombe
andiam preparar.

and that god, the sovereign
of the sea, be adored.
It is meet that we should celebrate
in dance and music.
(Soli)
From after he watches
Jove's anger
and in a moment
descends to the sea's depths,
where in his royal seat
he makes ready
and swiftly has his great
scaly steeds harnessed.

From out the waves
robust, jovial
herald tritons sound
their loud trumpets around.
Daylight returns,
for Neptune's great trident
has power to tame
the raging sea.

Neptune blows
on his golden shell,
his royal emblem.
Portunus, still an infant,
plays with his dolphin
and with Amphitrite.
He made us victorious
over the god of Hades.

Lovely nereids,
adorable nymphs
who with Galatea
form a court
to the great goddess,
o give our thanks
to those gods
who allowed us
to dry our eyes.
(Tutti)
Now let the trumpets sound
and us go to prepare
solemn sacrifice.

120

Atto secondo   Act two

SCENA PRIMA

Appartamenti reali.
Idomeneo, Arbace

RECITATIVO

IDOMENEO
Siam soli; odimi, Arbace,
e il grand' arcano in sen racchiudi.
Assai per lungo uso
m'è nota tua fedeltà.

ARBACE
Di fedeltà il vassallo merto non ha;
virtù non è il dover.
Ecco la vita, il sangue . . .

IDOMENEO
Un consiglio or mi fa d'uopo,
ascolta: tu sai quanto a Trojani fu il
brando mio fatal.

ARBACE
Tutto m'è noto.

IDOMENEO
Gonfio di tante imprese,
al varco alfin m'attese il fier
Nettuno.

ARBACE
E so, che a danni tuoi,
ad Eolo unito e a Giove,
il suo regno sconvolse.

SCENE 1

The royal apartments.
Idomeneo, Arbace

RECITATIVE

IDOMENEO
We are alone; listen, Arbace,
and lock my great secret in your breast.
Through long association
your loyalty is sufficiently known to me.

ARBACE
A vassal claims no credit for loyalty:
a duty is not a virtue.
Here is my life, my blood . . .

IDOMENEO
I need your advice now; listen: you
know how fatal my sword was to the
Trojans.

ARBACE
I know it well.

IDOMENEO
Jealous of such feats, proud Neptune
awaited me just before putting to
sea.

ARBACE
And I know that to harm you
he joined with Aeolus and Jove
and roused his kingdom.

121

IDOMENEO
Sì, che m'estorse in voto umana
vittima.

ARBACE
Di chi?

IDOMENEO
Del primo, che sulla spiaggia
incauto a me s'appressi.

ARBACE
Or dimmi, chi primo tu incontrasti?

IDOMENEO
Inorridisci . . . il mio figlio!

ARBACE
Idamante! Io vengo meno . . .
Ti vide? Il conoscesti?

IDOMENEO
Mi vide, e a offrir mi ogni sollievo
accorse, credendomi stranier,
e il morto padre piangendo,
al lungo ragionar
l'un l'altro conobbe alfin.
Ahi conoscenza . . .

ARBACE
A lui il suo destin svelasti?

IDOMENEO
No, che da orror confuso io m'involai,
disperato il lasciai.

ARBACE
Povero padre! Idamante infelice!

IDOMENEO
Dammi, Arbace, il consiglio,
salvami per pietà, salvami il figlio.

ARBACE
Trovisi in altro clima, altro
soggiorno.

IDOMENEO
Dura necessità! Ma dove mai, dove
ad occhio immortal potrà
celarsi?

IDOMENEO
Yes, he extorted from me, as tribute, a
human sacrifice.

ARBACE
Of whom?

IDOMENEO
Of the first person who should approach
me without warning on the beach.

ARBACE
Tell me then, whom did you first meet?

IDOMENEO
Steel yourself. . . . my son!

ARBACE
Idamante! I grow faint . . .
Did he see you? Did you recognise him?

IDOMENEO
He saw me, and hastened to offer me
all assistance, believing me a stranger,
and, lamenting his dead father,
he spoke at length.
Eventually we recognised each other.
Ah, what a realisation . . .

ARBACE
Did you reveal to him his fate?

IDOMENEO
No. for I fled, confounded with horror,
and left him in despair.

ARBACE
Poor father! Unhappy Idamante!

IDOMENEO
Give me advice, Arbace,
for pity's sake save my son for me!

ARBACE
He must find some other place to live, in
some other land.

IDOMENEO
Harsh necessity! But where in the world,
where could he hide from the immortals'
eyes?

122

ARBACE

urchè al popol si celi, per altra via
n tanto Nettuno si placherà,
ualch' altro Nume di lui cura
'avrà.

IDOMENEO

Ben dici, è vero . . .
Ilia s'appressa, ohimè!
n Argo ei vada, e sul paterno soglio
imetta Elettra . . .
Or vanne a lei, e al figlio;
a che sian pronti;
. tutto sollecito disponi,
ustodisci l'arcano, a te mi fido;
te dovranno, o caro, o fido Arbace,
a vita il figlio, e il genitor la pace.

0.   ARIA

ARBACE

e il tuo duol,
e il mio desio
e'nvolassero del pari,
ubbidirti qual son io,
aria il duol pronto a fuggir.
Quali al trono sian compagni,
hi l'ambiscè or veda e impari
tia lontan, o non si lagni,
e non trova che martir.
parte)

SCENA SECONDA

lia, Idomeneo

RECITATIVO

ILIA

e mai pomposo apparse
ull' Argivo orizzonte il dio di Delo
ccolo in questo giorno.
O sire, in cui l'augusta tua presenza
tuoi diletti sudditi torna in vita,
lor pupille, che ti piansero estinto,
or rasserena.

IDOMENEO

Principessa gentil, il bel sereno
nche alle tue pupille omai ritorni,

ARBACE

Provided he hid from the people, Neptune
could by other means be appeased
meantime; some other god could protect
him.

IDOMENEO

You counsel well; it is true . . .
Alas! Ilia approaches!
Let him go to Argos, and accompany
Electra to her native land . . .
So go to her, and to my son:
bid them make ready;
prepare everything with all speed,
and keep the secret I have confided to you;
to you, my dear loyal Arbace, we will owe
the son's life, the father's peace of mind.

10.   ARIA

ARBACE

If your grief
and my desire
to serve you as I can
are of equal measure,
your grief will quickly vanish.
He who is close to the throne
and aspires to it must watch
and learn to stay away, or not complain
if he finds here nothing but suffering.
(exit)

SCENE 2

Ilia, Idomeneo

RECITATIVE

ILIA

If ever the god of Delos appeared
in splendour on the Argive horizon,
he does so this day.
O sire, whose august presence restores
your beloved subjects to life,
you will comfort their eyes,
which mourned you as dead.

IDOMENEO

Gentle princess, let lovely serenity
return to your own eyes too;

123

il lungo duol dilegua.

ILIA
Io piansi, è vero, e in vano
l'are tue, o glauca Dea, bagnai.
Ecuba genitrice, ah tu lo sai,
piansi in veder l'antico Priamo genitor
dell' armi sotto al grave incarco,
al suo partir, al tristo avviso
di sua morte, e piansi poi
al vedere nel tempio il ferro,
il fuoco, la patria distrutta,
e me rapita in questa acerba età,
fra nemici e tempeste,
prigionera sotto un polo stranier . . .

IDOMENEO
Assai soffristi,
ma ogni trista memoria or si
sbandisca.

ILIA
Poichè il tuo amabil figlio libertà mi
donò di grazie e onori mi ricolmò,
tutta di tuoi la gioja un me
raccolta io sento.
Eccomi, accetta l'omaggio,
ed in tributo il mio,
non più infelice ma avventurato cor,
al figlio, al genitor, grato e divoto.
Signor! Umile è il don, sincero è il
voto.

IDOMENEO
Idamante mio figlio,
allor che libertà ti diè,
non fu che interprete felice
del paterno voler.
S'ei mi prevenne quanto ei fece
a tuo prò, tutto io confermo.
Di me, de' miei tesori Ilia disponi,
e mia cura sarà di darti chiare prove
dell' amicizia mia.

ILIA
Son certa, e un dubbio in me
colpa saria. Propizie stelle!
Qual benigno influsso la sorte mia
cangiò? Dove temei strazio e morte
incontrar, lieta rinasco; colgo dove
credei avverso il tutto dell' amare

end your long grief.

ILIA
I wept, it is true, and in vain my tears
bathed your altars, o goddess of the sea.
Hecuba, my mother, well you know it,
I wept to see my old father Priam
under the heavy burden of arms,
at his parting, at the sad news of his death
and then I wept to see
weapons in the temple,
the holocaust, my country destroyed,
and myself brought, at this bitter time,
amid foes and tempests,
a prisoner under a foreign sky . . .

IDOMENEO
You have suffered enough;
now let all your sad memories be
banished.

ILIA
Because your kind son gave me freedom
and showered me with honours,
I feel all your joy reflected in me.
Lo, accept my homage,
and in tribute take my heart,
tested but no longer unhappy,
grateful and devoted
to both son and father.
Sire, my gift is humble but my vow
sincere.

IDOMENEO
When my son Idamante
gave you your freedom
he was but the happy interpreter
of his father's will.
Though he forestalled me in what he did
to your advantage, I entirely confirm his
actions. Ilia, I and all I own are at your
disposal and it will be my concern to
offer you clear proof of my friendship.

ILIA
I am sure of it, and I would be wrong
to doubt it. Propitious stars!
What benign influence has changed my
lot? Where I feared to find torture and
death, I am reborn to happiness.
Where I expected the fullness of my bitte

mie pene il dolce frutto.

11. ARIA

ILIA
Se il padre perdei,
la patria, il riposo,
tu padre mi sei,
soggiorno amoroso
è Creta per me.
Or più non rammento
l'angoscie, gli affanni,
or gioja e contento,
compenso a miei danni,
il cielo mi die.
(parte)

SCENA TERZA

Idomeneo solo

RECITATIVO

IDOMENEO
Qual mi conturba i sensi equivoca
favella! Ne' suoi casi qual mostra a
un tratto in tempestiva gioja la
Frigia principessa? Quei ch'esprime
teneri sentimenti per il prence . . .
sarebber forse, ahimè, sentimenti
d'amor, gioja di speme? . . .
Non m'inganno, reciproco è l'amore.
Troppo, Idamante, a scior' quelle
catene sollecito tu fosti . . .
Ecco il delitto, che in te punisce il
ciel. Si, a Nettuno il figlio, il padre
ed Ilia, tre vittime saran sul' ara
istessa, da egual dolor afflitte: una
dal ferro e due dal duol trafitte.

12. ARIA

IDOMENEO
Fuor del mar ho un mar in seno,
che del primo è più funesto,
e Nettuno ancor in questo
mai non cessa minacciar.
Fiero Nume! Dimmi almeno
se al naufragio è si vicino
il mio cor, qual rio destino

sufferings, I gather sweet fruit,

11. ARIA

ILIA
If I have lost my father,
my country and my peace of mind,
you are now a father to me,
and Crete is for me
a blessed land to stay.
Now I recall no more
my anguish and distress;
now heaven has given me
joy and contentment
to compensate for my loss.
(exit)

SCENE 3

Idomeneo alone

RECITATIVE

IDOMENEO
How her ambiguous words disturb my
mind! Why does the Phrygian princess
suddenly, in her situation, show such
tempestuous joy? She expresses tender
feelings for the prince . . .
could they perhaps be, alas, feelings of
love, the joy of hope? . . .
I am not mistaken, their love is mutual.
Idamante, you were too quick
to loose those chains . . .
This was the crime for which heaven
punishes you. Yes, there will be three
victims for Neptune on the same altar,
afflicted with like pain — son, father and
Ilia, one pierced by the knife, two by grief.

12. ARIA

IDOMENEO
Saved from the sea, I still have a raging
sea more fearsome than before within my
bosom, and Neptune does not cease
his threats even in this.
Stern god! Tell me at least,
if my body was so close to shipwreck,
for what cruel purpose

or gli vieta il naufragar.

RECITATIVO

IDOMENEO
Frettolosa e giuliva Elettra vien:
s'ascolti.

SCENA QUARTA

Elettra, Idomeneo

ELETTRA
Sire, da Arbace intesi quanto
la tua clemenza s'interessa per me;
già all'infinito giunser
le grazie tue, l'obbligo mio.
Or, tua mercè, verdeggia in me
la speme di vedere ben tosto depresso
de' ribelli il folle orgoglio,
e come a tanto amore corrisponder
potrò?

IDOMENEO
Di tua difesa ha l'impegno Idamante.
A lui men' vado;
farò che adempia or'or l'intento mio,
il suo dover, e appaghi il tuo desio.
(parte)

ELETTRA
Chi mai del mio provò piacer più
dolce!

SCENA QUINTA

Elettra sola

ELETTRA
Parto, e l'unico oggetto ch'amo ed
adoró, O Dei, meco s'en vien?
Ah, troppo angusto è il mio cor
a tanta gioja!
Lunge della rivale farò ben io,
con vezzi e con lusinghe,
che quel foco che pria spegnere non
potei, a quei lumi s'estingua,
e avvampi ai miei.

that wreck was withheld.

RECITATIVE

IDOMENEO
Electra comes in happy haste:
I must hear her.

SCENE 4

Electra, Idomeneo

ELECTRA
Sire, from Arbace I learned how much,
in your graciousness, you favour me;
your kindness and my indebtedness
pass all bounds.
Now, thanks to you, hope rises in me
of seeing the insane ambition
of the vanquished soon crushed;
how can I repay you for such
love?

IDOMENEO
Idamante is pledged to defend you.
To him I am going;
to bid him at once fulfil my intent
and his duty, and to satisfy your wish.
(exit)

ELECTRA
What sweeter pleasure than mine was
ever felt?

SCENE 5

Electra alone

ELECTRA
I leave, and the one being I love
and adore, o gods, comes with me?
Ah, my heart cannot contain such joy!
Away from my rival, I shall succeed
with caresses and endearments,
so that the fire I could not quench before
no longer burns for her eyes
but blazes for
mine.

13. ARIA

ELETTRA
Idol mio, se ritroso
altro amante a me ti rende,
non m'offende rigoroso,
più m'alletta austero amor.
Scaccierà vicino ardore
dal tuo sen l'ardor lontano;
più la mano può d'amore
s'è vicin l'amante cor.

14. MARCIA

Odo da lunge armonioso suono,
che mi chiama all'imbarco, orsù si
vada.
(parte)

SCENA SESTA

*Il porto di Sidone, con bastimenti
lungo le spiagge.*
Elettra, Coro

RECITATIVO

ELETTRA
Sidonie sponde, o voi per me
di pianto e duol, d'amor!
Nemico crudo ricetto,
or ch'astro più clemente
a voi mi toglie, io vi perdono,
e in pace allieto partir mio
alfin vi lascio e do l'estremo addio.

15. CORO

Placido è il mar; andiamo,
tutto ci rassicura,
felice avrem ventura;
sù, sù, partiamo or' or!

ELETTRA
Soavi Zeffiri soli spirate,
del freddo horea l'ira calmate,
d'aura piacevole cortesi siate,
se da voi spargesi per tutto amor.

13. ARIA

ELECTRA
My dearest, if reluctantly
your other lover yields you to me,
constrained love does not deter me,
and your coldness is more alluring to me.
Passion close at hand will drive
from your heart more distant fires;
the hand of love has more power
when the beloved is near.

14. MARCH

In the distance I hear the sweet sound
summoning me aboard; well then, I must
go.
(exit)

SCENE 6

*The port of Sidon, with ships along the
shore*
Electra, chorus

RECITATIVE

ELECTRA
Shores of Sidon, you hostile, harsh spot
which saw my tears, my grief, my love,
now that a more compassionate star
takes me from you,
I forgive you;
I go in peace and gladness,
leave you at last, and say a final farewell.

15. CHORUS

The sea is calm; let us go;
everything is reassuring;
we shall have good fortune;
come, let us leave at once!

ELECTRA
Blow, gentle breezes only;
calm the anger of the icy north wind;
be generous with your pleasing breath
which spreads love everywhere.

127

SCENA SETTIMA

Idomeneo, Idamante e detti

RECITATIVO

IDOMENEO
Vatene prence.

IDAMANTE
O ciel!

IDOMENEO
Troppo t'arresti.
Parti, e non dubbia fama
di mille eroiche imprese
il tuo ritorno prevenga:
di regnare se l'arte apprender vuoi,
ora incomincia a renderti
de' miseri il sostegno,
del padre e di te stesso
ognor più degno.

16. TERZETTO

IDAMANTE
Pria di partir, O Dio,
soffri che unbacio imprima
sulla paterna man.

ELETTRA
Soffri che un grato addio
sul labbro il cor esprima;
addio, degno sovran.

IDOMENEO
(a Elettra)
Vanne, sarai felice.
(a Idamante)
Figlio, tua sorte è questa.
Seconda i voti, o ciel!

A TRE
Seconda i voti, o ciel!

ELETTRA
Quanto sperar mi lice!

IDAMANTE
(Vado, e il mio cor qui resta.)
Addio!

128

SCENE 7

Idomeneo, Idamante and the above

RECITATIVE

IDOMENEO
Go then, prince.

IDAMANTE
O heaven!

IDOMENEO
You tarry too long.
Go, and let the clear fame
of a thousand heroic deeds
herald your return.
If you wish to learn the art of ruling,
begin now by giving
help to the unfortunate,
and becoming ever more worthy
of your father and yourself.

16. TRIO

IDAMANTE
Before leaving, allow me,
O gods, to place a kiss
on my father's hand.

ELECTRA
Let my heart express through my lips
a grateful farewell;
farewell, noble king.

IDOMENEO
(to Electra)
Go then and be happy.
(to Idamante)
This is your lot, my son.
Answer our prayer, o heaven!

ALL THREE
Answer our prayer, o heaven!

ELECTRA
How great are my hopes!

IDAMANTE
(I go, but my heart remains here.)
Farewell!

A TRE

Addio!

ALL THREE

Farewell!

IDOMENEO & IDAMANTE
Destin crudel!

IDOMENEO & IDAMANTE
Cruel destiny!

IDAMANTE
(O Ilia!)

IDAMANTE
(O Ilia!)

IDOMENEO
(O figlio!)

IDOMENEO
(My son!)

IDAMANTE
O padre! O partenza!

IDAMANTE
My father! To part!

ELETTRA
O dei! Che sarà?

ELECTRA
Ye gods, what will happen?

A TRE
Deh cessi il scompiglio,
del ciel la clemenza sua, man
porgerà.

ALL THREE
O may this agitation cease
and heaven stretch out a hand in
compassion.

*(Mentre vanno ad imbacarsi sorge
improviso tempesta)*

*(As they are about to embark, a storm
suddenly springs up)*

17. CORO

17. CHORUS

Qual nuovo terrore! Qual rauco
mugito! De' Numi il furore ha il mar
infierito. Nettuno, mercè!

What new terror is this? What hoarse
roaring! The gods' fury has whipped up
the sea. Neptune, have mercy!

*(Incalza la tempesta, il mare si
gonfia, il cielo tuona e lampeggia.
Un mostro formidable s'appresenta
fuori dell' onde.)*

*(The storm increases, the sea rises;
thunder and lightning. A terrible monster
appears from out of the
sea.)*

Qual' odio, qual' ira Nettuno ci
mostra, se il cielo s'adira, qual colpoè
la nostra? Il reo qual'e?

What hate, what anger Neptune shows us!
What is our sin, that heaven rages?
Who is the guilty one?

RECITATIVO

RECITATIVE

IDOMENEO
Eccoti in me, barbaro Nume! Il reo!
Io solo errai, me sol punisci,
e cada sopra di me il tuo sdegno.
La mia morte ti sazi alfin;
ma se altra aver pretendi
vittima al fallo mio,

IDOMENEO
Here he is, cruel god! I am the guilty one!
I alone have sinned; punish me alone
and let your wrath fall on me.
May my death at last satisfy you;
but if you claim
another victim for my fault,

129

una innocente darti io non posso,
e se pur tu la vuoi . . .
ingiusto sei, pretenderla non puoi.

18. CORO

Corriamo, fuggiamo
quel mostro spietato!
Ah, preda gia siamo!
Chi, perfido fato,
più crudo è di te?

I cannot give you an innocent one,
yet if you demand him . . .
you are unjust, and cannot claim him.

18. CHORUS

Let us run, let us fly
from that pitiless monster!
Ah, we are already his prey!
Treacherous fate, who
is more cruel than you?

Atto   terzo

Act three

SCENA PRIMA

Giardino reale.
Ilia sola

RECITATIVO

ILIA
Solitudini amiche, aure amorose,
piante fiorite e fiori vaghi!
Udite d'una infelice amante i
lamenti, che a voi lassa confido.
Quanto il tacer prosso al mio
vincitore, quanto il fingerti costa
afflitto core!

19.   ARIA

ILIA
Zeffiretti lusinghieri,
deh volate al mio tesoro,
e gli dite ch'io l'adoro,
che mi serbi il cor fedel.
E voi piante, e fior sinceri,
che ora inaffia il pianto amaro,
dite a lui, che amor più raro
mai vedeste sotto al ciel.

RECITATIVO

ILIA
Ei stesso vien . . . O Dei!
Mi spiego o taccio?
Resto . . . parto . . . o m'ascondo?
Ah, risolver non posso, mi confondo!

SCENE 1

The royal garden.
Ilia alone

RECITATIVE

ILIA
Friendly solitudes, amorous breezes,
blossoming plants and lovely flowers,
hearken to the laments of an unhappy
lover who, forsaken, confides in you.
How much it costs my afflicted heart to
keep silent and pretend, when close to
him who conquered it!

19.   ARIA

ILIA
Gently caressing zephyrs,
o fly to my beloved
and tell him I adore him
and that my heart will remain faithful.
And you plants and tender flowers
which my bitter tears water,
tell him that you never saw
a love more rare beneath the sky.

RECITATIVE

ILIA
He himself is coming . . . O heaven!
Shall I speak or be silent?
Shall I remain, or leave, or hide?
Ah, I cannot decide! I am confused!

131

SCENA SECONDA

Idamante, Ilia

IDAMANTE
Principessa, a tuoi sguardi
se offrirmi ardisco ancor,
più non mi guida
un temerario affetto;
altro or non cerco,
che appagarti e morir.

ILIA
Morir? Tu, prence?

IDAMANTE
Più teco io resto,
più di te m'accendo,
e s'aggrava mia colpa;
a che il castigo più a lungo differir?

ILIA
Ma qual cagione morte a cercar
t'induce?

IDAMANTE
Il genitore pien di smania
e furore torvo mi guarda
e fugge, e il motivo mi cela;
da tue catene avvinto, il tuo rigore
a nuovi guai m'espone.
Un fiero mostro fa
dapertutto orrida strage;
or questo a combatter si vada
e vincerlo si tenti;
O finisca la morte i miei tormenti!

ILIA
Calma, o prence, un trasporto sì
funesto; rammenta, che tu sei
d'un grand' impero l'unica speme.

IDAMANTE
Privo, del tuo amore,
privo, Ilia, di te,
nulla mi cale.

ILIA
Misera me! . . . Deh serba i giorni
tuoi!

SCENE 2

Idamante, Ilia

IDAMANTE
Princess, if I still dare
to offer myself to your sight,
a bold passion
no longer guides me;
now I seek no more than to ask
your forgiveness, and to die.

ILIA
Die? You, prince?

IDAMANTE
The more I stay with you,
the more I am afire for you,
and my guilt increases:
why further postpone the punishment?

ILIA
But what reason impels you to seek
death?

IDAMANTE
My father, filled with fury
and anger, gazes at me grimly
and flees, giving me no reason.
Bound by your chains, your severity
exposes me to new woes.
A savage monster wreaks
dreadful havoc far and wide;
now I must go to fight it
and try to destroy it;
o let death end my torments!

ILIA
O prince, calm this melancholy ferment;
recall that you are
the sole hope of a great empire.

IDAMANTE
Without your love,
without you, Ilia,
nothing matters to me.

ILIA
Poor me! . . . O preserve your
life!

IDAMANTE
Il mio fato crudel seguir degg'io.

ILIA
Vivi . . . Ilia te'l chiede.

IDAMANTE
O Dei! Che ascolto?
Principessa adorata!

ILIA
Il cor turbato a te mal custodi
la debolezza mia; pur troppo amore,
e tema indivisi ho nel sen.

IDAMANTE
Odo? O sol quel che brama finge
l'udito? O pure il grand' ardore
m'agita i sensi, e il cor lusinga
oppresso un dolce sogno?

ILIA
Ah! Perchè pria non arsi,
che scoprir la mia fiamma?
Mille io sento rimorsi all'alma.
Il sacro mio dovere,
la mia gloria, la patria,
il sangue de' miei ancor fumante,
oh quanto al core rimproverano
il mio ribelle amore!
Ma alfin, che fo?
Già che in periglio estremo
ti vedo, o caro,
e trarti sola io posso,
odimi, io te'l ridico:
t'amo! t'adoro!
E se morir tu vuoi,
pria che m'uccida il duol
morir non puoi.

20. DUETTO

IDAMANTE
S'io non moro a questi accenti,
non è ver che amor uccida,
che la gioja opprima un cor.

ILIA
Non più duol, non più lamenti!
Io ti son constante e fida,
tu sei il solo mio tesor!

IDAMANTE
I must follow my cruel fate.

ILIA
No, live . . . Ilia implores you.

IDAMANTE
O gods, what do I hear?
Adored princess!

ILIA
My troubled heart cannot conceal from
you my weakness; in my breast I have
both too much love and fear.

IDAMANTE
Do I hear alright? Or does my hearing only
imagine what it longs for? Or does my
ardent passion excite my senses so that a
sweet dream flatters my oppressed heart?

ILIA
Ah, why did I not perish
before disclosing my passion?
My soul is overwhelmed with remorse.
My sacred duty,
my honour, my country,
my kinsmen's blood still hot,
oh how they reproach
the rebellious love in my heart!
But what can I do?
Now that I see you
in deadly danger, my dearest,
and only I can save you,
hear me, I tell you again:
I love you! I adore you!
And if you wish to die,
grief will already have killed me
before you can do so.

20. DUET

IDAMANTE
If I do not die at these words
it is not true that love can kill
and that joy oppresses the heart.

ILIA
No more grief, no more lamenting!
I will be constant and true to you;
you are my only treasure!

IDAMANTE
Tu sarai la mia sposa.

IDAMANTE
You shall be my wife.

ILIA
Qual tu mi vuoi, lo sposo mio sarai
tu!

ILIA
As you desire me, you shall be my
husband!

IDAMANTE & ILIA
Lo dica Amor!
Ah, il gioir sorpassa in noi
il sofferto affanno rio;
tutto vince il nostro ardor.

IDAMANTE & ILIA
Let love speak!
Ah, our joy banishes
the cruel torments we have suffered;
our love is all-conquering.

SCENA TERZA

Vengono Idomeneo ed Elettra

RECITATIVO

SCENE 3

Enter Idomeneo and Electra

RECITATIVE

IDOMENEO
(Cieli! Che vedo?)

IDOMENEO
(Heavens! What do I see?)

ILIA
Ah, siam scoperti, o caro.

ILIA
Ah, we are discovered, beloved!

IDAMANTE
Non temer, idol mio.

IDAMANTE
Do not fear, my love.

ELETTRA
(Ecco l'ingrato . . .)

ELECTRA
(Ungrateful Idamante!)

IDOMENEO
Io ben m'apposi al ver.
Ah crudo fato!

IDOMENEO
I suspected the truth.
Ah harsh fate!

IDAMANTE
Signor, già più non oso padre
chiamarti, a un suddito infelice deh
questa almen concedi unica grazia.

IDAMANTE
My lord — I dare no longer call you father
— I pray you, grant one favour to your
unhappy subject.

IDOMENEO
Parla.

IDOMENEO
Speak.

ELETTRA
Che dirà?

ELECTRA
What will he say?

IDAMANTE
In che t'offesi mai?
Perchè mi fuggi,
m'odi e aborisci?

IDAMANTE
In what have I ever offended you?
Why do you fly from me,
hate me and shun me?

ILIA
Io tremo.

ELETTRA
Io tel direi.

IDOMENEO
Figlio, contro di me
Nettuno irato gelommi il cor;
ogni tua tenerezza
l'affanno mio raddoppia,
il tuo dolore tutto sul cor
mi piomba, e rimirarti
senza ribrezzo e orror non posso.

ILIA
O Dio!

IDAMANTE
Forse per colpa mia Nettun
sdegnossi; ma la colpa qual'è?

IDOMENEO
Ah, placarlo potessi senza di te!

ELETTRA
(Ah, potessi i torti miei or vindicar!)

IDOMENEO
Parti, te lo comando! Fuggi il
paterno lido e cerca altrove sicuro
asilo.

ILIA
Ahimè! Pietosa principessa,
ah mi conforta!

ELETTRA
Ch'io ti conforti? E come?
(Ancor m'insulta l'indegna.)

IDAMANTE
Dunque io me n'andrò!
Ma dove? . . . O Ilia! O genitor!

ILIA
O seguirti o morir, mio ben voglio.

ILIA
I tremble.

ELECTRA
And so you should.

IDOMENEO
My son, Neptune, incensed against me,
has frozen my heart;
all your tenderness
doubles my torment,
all your sorrow weighs
on my heart, and I cannot look at you
without a shudder of horror.

ILIA
O God!

IDAMANTE
Perhaps it is my fault that Neptune is
wroth; but what is my offence?

IDOMENEO
Ah, could I but placate him without you!

ELECTRA
(Ah, could I now avenge my wrongs!)

IDOMENEO
Leave, I command you! Flee your native
shore and seek safe refuge
elsewhere.

ILIA
Alas! Compassionate princess,
comfort me!

ELECTRA
I comfort you? How?
(She shamelessly insults me still further.)

IDAMANTE
Then I must go!
But whither? . . . O Ilia! O father!

ILIA
I desire to follow you, beloved, or to die.

IDAMANTE
Deh resta, o cara, e vivi in pace.
Addio!

IDAMANTE
O remain here, my dearest, and live in
peace. Farewell!

21.   QUARTETTO

21.   QUARTET

IDAMANTE
Andrò ramingo e solo,
morte cercando altrove,
finchè la incontrerò.

IDAMANTE
I will go on my wanderings alone,
seeking death elsewhere
until I find it.

ILIA
M'avrai compagna al duolo
dove sarai, e dove
tu moja, io morirò.

ILIA
You will have me as companion in your
grief wherever you go, and where you die
I too will die.

IDAMANTE
Ah no!

IDAMANTE
Ah no!

IDOMENEO
Nettun spietato!
Chi per pietà m'uccide?

IDOMENEO
Pitiless Neptune!
Who, in mercy, will take my life?

ELETTRA
(Quando vendetta avrò?)

ELECTRA
(When shall I be revenged?)

IDAMANTE & ILIA
(ad Idomeneo)
Serena il ciglio irato,
ah, il cor mi si divide.

IDAMANTE & ILIA
(to Idomeneo)
Calm your angry brow;
ah, my heart is breaking.

A QUATTRO
Soffrir più non si può.
Peggio è di morte
si gran dolore.
Più fiera sorte,
pena maggiore,
nessun provò.
(parte Idamante)

ALL FOUR
To suffer more is impossible.
Such great grief
is worse than death.
No one has ever suffered
a harsher fate
or greather punishment.
(exit Idamante)

SCENA QUARTA

SCENE 4

Viene Arbace

Enter Arbace

RECITATIVO

RECITATIVE

ARBACE
Sire, all reggia tua immensa turba
di popolo affollato
ad alta voce parlar ti chiede.

ARBACE
Sire, at your palace a vast crowd
is gathered, loudly clamouring
for you to speak.

136

LIA
A qualche nuovo affanno
preparati, mio cor.)

IDOMENEO
Perduto è il figlio!)

ARBACE
Del Dio de' mari
il sommo sacerdote la guida.

IDOMENEO
Ahi, troppo disperato è il caso!)
Intesi, Arbace.

ELETTRA
Qual nuovo disastro?

ILIA
Il popol sollevato?

IDOMENEO
Or vado ad ascoltarla.
(esce)

ELETTRA
Ti seguirò.
(esce)

ILIA
Voglio seguirti anch'io.
(esce)

SCENA QUINTA

Arbace solo

ARBACE
Sventurata Sidon! In te quai miro
di morte, stragi e orror lugubri
aspetti? Ah, Sidon più non sei,
sei la città del pianto,
e questa reggia quella del duol.
Dunque è per noi
dal cielo sbandita ogni pietà?
Chi sa? Io spero ancora . . .
che qualche Nume amico
si plachi a tanto sangue;
un Nume solo basta tutti a piegar.
Alla clemenza il rigor cederà . . .
Ma ancor non scorgo

ILIA
(Prepare yourself, my heart
for some new distress.)

IDOMENEO
(My son is lost!)

ARBACE
The High Priest of Neptune
is at their head.

IDOMENEO
(Alas, the situation is desperate!)
I understand, Arbace.

ELECTRA
What new disaster?

ILIA
Are the people rebelling?

IDOMENEO
I go now to hear them.
(exit)

ELECTRA
I will follow you.
(exit)

ILIA
I will go with you too.
(exit)

SCENE 5

Arbace alone

ARBACE
Unhappy Sidon, what gloomy aspects
of destruction, horror and death do I see
in you? Ah, you are no longer Sidon,
you are the city of tears
and this palace that of sorrow.
Then does heaven
deny us all pity?
Who knows? I still hope . . .
that some friendly god
will be satisfied with so much blood;
a single god could save us from all this.
Severity would yield to clemency . . .
But as yet I do not know

137

qual ci miri pietoso.
Ah, sordo è il cielo!
Ah, Creta tutta io vedo
finir sua gloria sotto alte rovine!
No, sue miserie pria non avran fine.

who would look on us with pity.
Ah, heaven is deaf!
I see all Crete
ending her glory deep in ruins!
No, ere this her miseries will not be ended

22. ARIA

ARBACE
Se colà ne' fati è scritto,
Creta, o Dei, s'è rea, or cada;
paghi il fio del suo delitto,
ma salvate il prence, il rè.
Deh d'un sol vi plachi il sangue . . .
ecco il mio, se il mio v'aggrada . . .
e il bel regno, che già langue,
giusti Dei, abbia mercè!

22. ARIA

ARBACE
If thus it is written in our fate,
if Crete is guilty, ye gods, let her now fall
let her pay the penalty for her guilt,
but save the prince, the king.
Ah, let the blood of one alone appease yo
here is mine, if mine will content you . . .
and have pity, just gods,
on the fair kingdom which is grieving!

SCENA SESTA

*Gran piazza avanti al palazzo reale.
Idomeneo, accompagnato d'Arbace
e del seguito reale, si siede sopra un
trono; il gran sacerdote, sacerdoti e
popolo.*

SCENE 6

*A large square in front of the royal pal-
ace. Idomeneo, accompanied by Arbace
and the royal retinue, is sitting on a thron
throne. The High Priest, priests and
people.*

23. RECITATIVO

GRAN SACERDOTE
Volgi intorno lo sguardo, o Sire,
e vedi qual strage orrenda
nel tuo nobil regno
fa il crudo mostro!
Ah, mira allagate di sangue
quelle publiche vie!
Ad ogni passo vedrai chi geme,
e l'alma gonfio d'ato velen
dal corpo esala.
Mille e mille in quell'ampio
sozzo ventre pria sepolti,
che morti perire io stesso vidi;
sempré di sangue lorde
son quelle fauci,
e son sempre ingorde.
Da te solo dipende il ripiego,
da morte trar tu puoi
il resto del tuo popolo,
ch'esclama sbigottito,
e da te l'aiuto implora,
e indugi ancor?

23. RECITATIVE

HIGH PRIEST
Gaze around you, sire,
and see what dreadful devastation
the savage monster has wrought
in your noble kingdom!
Behold the pools of blood
in the public streets!
At every step you will see someone
groaning, giving up the ghost from a body
swollen with black poison.
Thousands upon thousands lie dead and
buried in that immense and hideous belly
whom I myself saw perish.
That maw is foul with blood
and ever greedy.

On you alone depends our fate;
only you can save
from death the rest of your people,
who cry out in despair
and implore your help;
yet you still hesitate?

Al tempio, Sire . . .
Qual'è, dov'è la vittima?
A Nettuno rendi quello ch'è suo.

IDOMENEO
Non più! Sacro ministro, e voi popoli,
udite: la vittima è Idamante . . .
e or' or vedrete, o Numi, con qual
ciglio svenar il genitor il proprio
figlio.
(parte)

24. CORO

O voto tremendo!
Spettacolo orrendo!
Già regna la morte,
d'abisso le porte
spalanca crudel.

GRAN SACERDOTE
O cielo clemente!
Il figlio è innocente,
il voto è inumano;
arresta la mano
del padre fedel.
(partono tutti dolenti)

SCENA SETTIMA

*Veduta esteriore dal magnifico
tempio di Nettuno; la statua del dio
in fondo. I sacerdoti preparono il
sacrificio.*

25. MARCIA

*Arriva Idomeneo accompagnato da
numeroso seguito. Il gran sacerdote.*

26. IDOMENEO, poi SACERDOTI

Accogli, o rè del mar,
i nostri voti;
placa lo sdegno tuo,
il tuo rigor!

IDOMENEO
Tornino a lor spelonche
gli euri, i noti;

Sir, to the temple . . .
Who is the victim, and where is he?
Render unto Neptune that which is his.

IDOMENEO
No more! Holy priest, and my people,
listen: the victim is Idamante . . .
now you shall see, o gods, with what
bearing a father slays his own
son.
(exit)

24. CHORUS

O terrible vow!
Dreadful sight!
Death now reigns,
and opens wide the gates
of the fearful abyss.

HIGH PRIEST
O merciful heaven!
The son is innocent
and the vow inhuman;
stay the hand
of this pious father.
(exeunt omnes in sorrow)

SCENE 7

*The exterior of the magnificent temple of
Neptune; the statue of the god in the
background. The priests are preparing
the sacrifice.*

25. MARCH

*Enter Idomeneo, accompanied by a large
retinue. The High Priest.*

26. IDOMENEO, then PRIESTS

O king of the sea, receive
our prayers;
abate your anger,
your severity!

IDOMENEO
Let the east and south winds
return to their caves:

torni zeffiro al mar,
cessi il furor!
Il pentimento, e il cor
de' tuoi devòti
accetta e a noi concedi
il tuo favor.

CORO
(dentro le scene)
Stupenda vittoria!
Eterna è tua gloria!
Trionfa, o signor!

RECITATIVO

IDOMENEO
Qual risuona qui intorno
applauso di vittoria?

SCENA OTTAVA

Arbace e detti

ARBACE
Sire, il prence, Idamante l'eroe,
di morte in traccia disperato
correndo, il trionfo trovò.
Sull' empio mostro scogliossi
furibondo, il vinse e uccise.
Eccoci salvi alfin.

IDOMENEO
Ahimè, Nettuno di nuovo sdegno
acceso sarà contro di noi.
Or' or Arbace con tuo dolo vedrai
che Idamante trovò quel che cercava,
e di morte egli stesso il trionfo sarà.

ARBACE
Che vedo? O Numi!

SCENA NONA

*Idamante in veste bianca con
ghirlanda di fiori in capo,
circondato da guardie e da sacerdoti.
Popolo e detti.*

let the gentle breeze return to the sea
and the fury cease!
Accept the heartfelt
repentance of your devotees,
and grant us
your favour.

CHORUS
(within)
Resounding victory!
Eternal is your glory!
Triumph, o lord!

RECITATIVE

IDOMENEO
What is this applause of victory
which resounds about me?

SCENE 8

Arbace and the above

ARBACE
Sire, the prince, heroic Idamante,
in despair courting death
has triumphed over it.
He threw himself furiously upon the
savage monster, overcame it and killed it.
We are saved at last.

IDOMENEO
Alas, Neptune will be moved
to new fury against us.
Now, Arbace, to your sorrow you will see
that Idamante found what he was seeking,
and he himself will be death's booty.

ARBACE
What do I see? O ye gods!

SCENE 9

*Idamante in a white robe, with a
garland of flowers in his head, surrounded
by guards and priests. The populace; the
above.*

IDAMANTE
Padre, mio caro padre! Ah dolce
nome! Eccomi a piedi tuoi; in
questo estremo periodo fatal, su
quella destra, che il varco al sangue
tuo nelle mie vene aprir dovrà,
gli ultimi baci accetta.
Ora comprendo che il tuo
turbamento sdegno non era già, ma
amor paterno. O mille volte e mille
fortunato Idamante, se chi vita ti diè,
vita ti toglie, e togliendola a te la
rende al cielo, e dal cielo sua in
cambio impetra, ed impetra
costante a suoi la pace e de' Numi
l'amor sacro e verace.

IDOMENEO
O figlio! O caro figlio! Perdona:
il crudo uffizio in me scelta non è,
pena è del fato,
barbaro, iniquo fato!
Ah no, non posso contro un figlio
innocente alzar l'aspra bipenne;
da ogni fibra già sen' fuggon le
forze, e gli occhi miei torbida notte
ingombra. O figlio!

IDAMANTE
O padre! Ah, non t'arresti
inutile pietà; ne vana ti lusinghi
tenerezza d'amor.
Deh vibra un colpo,
che ambi toglia d'affanno.

IDOMENEO
Ah, che natura me'l contrasta e
ripugna.

IDAMANTE
Ceda natura al suo autor;
di Giove questo è l'alto voler.
Rammenta il tuo dover:
se un figlio perdi,
cento avrai Numi amici;
figli tuoi, i tuoi popoli sono . . .
Ma se in mia vece
brami che t'ubbidisca ed ami,
chi ti sia accanto
e di tue cure il peso teco ne porti,
Ilia ti raccomando.

IDAMANTE
Father, my dear father! Oh sweet name!
Behold me at your feet! In this last
fatal moment, before your hand must
strike the blow that empties your blood,
from my veins,
accept a last kiss.
Now I realise that your agitation
arose not from anger but from paternal
love. A thousand times fortunate is
Idamante if he who gave him life takes
life from him, and taking it, offers it to
heaven, that in exchange heaven may
ensure his own and he obtain lasting peace
for his people and the sacred and true love
of the gods.

IDOMENEO
My son! My dear son! Forgive me:
this dreadful task is not my choice,
but ordained by fate —
barbarous, inhuman fate!
Ah no, I cannot raise the brutal axe
against my innocent son;
strength fades from every fibre of my
being, and dark night clouds my eyes.
O my son!

IDAMANTE
O father! Do not let useless pity
stop you, nor the vain fondness
of love beguile you.
Let the blow fall
that will relieve us both of our distress.

IDOMENEO
Ah, how nature opposes me and abhors
this.

IDAMANTE
Nature must yield to her creator;
this is the mighty will of Jove.
Remember your duty:
though you lose a son
you will gain a hundred friendly gods;
your people are your sons . . .
But if in my stead
you desire one to obey and love you,
who will be near you
and share the burden of your cares,
I commend Ilia to you.

Deh un figlio tu esaudisci,
che moribondo, supplica e consiglia;
s'ella sposa non m'è, deh sia ti
figlia.

27. ARIA

IDAMANTE
No, la morte io non pavento,
se alla patria, al genitore frutta,
o Numi, il vostro amore
e di pace il bel seren.
Agli Elisi andrò contento,
e riposo avrà quest' alma,
se in lasciare la mia salma
vita e pace avrà mio ben.

RECITATIVO

IDAMANTE
Ma, che più tardi? Eccomi pronto;
adempi il sacrifizio, il voto.

IDOMENEO
Oh qual mi sento in ogni vena
insolito vigor . . . or risoluto son . . .
l'ultimo amplesso ricevi . . . e mori . .

IDAMANTE
O padre!

IDOMENEO
O figlio!

IDAMANTE & IDOMENEO
O Dio!

IDAMANTE
O Ilia, ohimè! Vivi felice, addio!

SCENA DECIMA

*Nel atto di ferire sopraviene Ilia ed
impedisce il colpo*

ILIA
Ferma, o Sire, che fai?

IDOMENEO
La vittima io sveno, che promisi a
Nettuno.

Ah, heed your son, who,
about to die, pleads and counsels:
if she cannot be my bride, let her be your
daughter.

27. ARIA

IDAMANTE
No, I do not fear death,
ye gods, if your love bestows
the sweet calm of peace on my
country and my father,
I will go contentedly to the Elysian fields
and my soul find rest
on leaving my body if my loved one
may have life and peace.

RECITATIVE

IDAMANTE
But why delay further? I am ready:
make the sacrifice, fulfil your vow.

IDOMENEO
O how I feel unwonted strength
in every vein . . . now I am resolved . . .
receive my last embrace . . . and die . . .

IDAMANTE
O father!

IDOMENEO
My son!

IDAMANTE & IDOMENEO
O God!

IDAMANTE
Alas, Ilia! Be happy, and farewell!

SCENE 10

*As Idomeneo is about to strike, Ilia inter-
venes and prevents the blow*

ILIA
Stop sire! What are you doing?

IDOMENEO
I must sacrifice the victim I promised to
Neptune.

IDAMANTE Ilia, t'achetta.	IDAMANTE Ilia, be calm.
GRAN SACERDOTE Deh non turbar il sacrifizio.	HIGH PRIEST Do not disturb the sacrifice.
ILIA Invano quella scure altro petto tenta ferir. Eccoti, Sire, il mio, la vittima io son.	ILIA In vain that axe attempts to wound another's breast. Here is mine, sire; I am your victim.
ELETTRA (O qual contrasto!)	ELECTRA (What an unexpected turn!)
ILIA Innocente è Idamante; è figlio tuo e del regno è la speme; tiranni i dei non son, fallaci siete interprete voi tutti del divino voler; vuol sgombrar il cielo de' nemici la Grecia e non de' figli; benchè innocente anch'io, benchè ora amica, di Priamo son figlia; e Frigia io nacqui, per natura nemica al greco nome. Orsù mi svena . . .	ILIA Idamante is innocent; he is your son and the hope of the kingdom; the gods are not tyrants, and you all wrongly interpret the divine will; heaven wishes to dispose of the enemies of Greece, not of her sons; although I too am innocent and now a friend, I am the daughter of Priam and was born a Phrygian, by nature a foe to the name of Greece. So kill me . . .
IDAMANTE Ah troppo, Ilia, sei generosa! Vittima si preziosa il genitore non promise. A Nettun me scelse il fato; la Frigia in te ancor vivo; chi sa a qual fine il ciel ti serba in vita e della Grecia in sen?	IDAMANTE Ah, Ilia, you are too generous! My father did not promise so precious a victim. Fate chose me for Neptune; Phrygia lives on in you; who knows to what end heaven has preserved your life in Greece's bosom?
ILIA Invan m'alletti.	ILIA You entreat me in vain.
IDAMANTE Invan morir presumi.	IDAMANTE In vain do you insist on dying.
IDOMENEO Ah, ch'io son fuor di me; soccorso, o Numi!	IDOMENEO Ah, I cannot bear it; help, ye gods!
ARBACE O ciel, che fia? Mi scoppia il cor.	ARBACE O heaven, what will happen? My heart is breaking.

ELETTRA	ELECTRA

ELETTRA
In petto quai moti ardenti
io sento di rabbia e di furor!

ELECTRA
What burning emotions of rage and fury
I feel in my breast!

GRAN SACERDOTE
Sire, risolvi omai . . .

HIGH PRIEST
Sire, decide now . . .

IDOMENEO
(ad Ilia)
Ma quella tu non sei . . .

IDOMENEO
(to Ilia)
But you are not the one . . .

ILIA
Sempre più grata è a Dei
vittima volontaria.

ILIA
A willing victim
is always more acceptable to the gods.

IDAMANTE
Idolo mio! Deh dammi
del tuo amor l'ultimo pegno.

IDAMANTE
My beloved! Ah, give me
a last pledge of your love.

ILIA
Ecco il mio sangue.

ILIA
I offer my blood.

IDAMANTE
Ah no, la gloria in pace lasciami
di morire per la mia patria.

IDAMANTE
Ah no, leave me the glory
of dying in peace for my country.

ILIA
A me s'aspetta . . . gratitudine è in
me . . . ma ti dispensa amore.
Nettun! Eccoti il mio.
*(Corre all'ara, vuole inghinocchiarsi,
Idamante la ritiene)*

ILIA
I am the appointed one . . . my gratitude
is great . . . but my love reprieves you.
Neptune, here is my blood!
*(She runs to the altar and is about to
kneel, but Idamante holds her back)*

IDAMANTE
O Dio! In me è dover!
O vivi e parti,
o insiem noi moriremo.

IDAMANTE
O god! My duty calls!
O live and go now,
or we shall die together.

ILIA
No, sola io vuo varcare il guado
estremo; a te, sacro ministro . . .
*(S'inghinoccia avanti al gran
sacerdote. S'ode gran strepito
sotteraneo; la statua di Nettuno si
scuote; il gran sacerdote si trova
avanti l'ara in estasi. Una voce
profonda e grave pronunzia la
seguente sentenza del cielo)*

ILIA
No, I wish to cross the last stream alone;
now, holy priest . . .
*(She kneels before the High Priest. A loud
noise is heard underground; Neptune's
statue shakes; the High Priest is in
ecstasy before the altar. A deep and
solemn voice makes the following
pronouncement from
heaven)*

28. LA VOCE

Ha vinto Amore . . .
A Idomeneo perdona il gran
trascorso il ciel, ma non al rè.
A lui mancar non lice a sue promesse.
Cessi esser rè; lo sia Idamante,
ed Ilia a lui sia sposa . . .
e fia pago Nettuno,
contento il ciel, premiata l'innocenza.
La pace renderà di Creta al regno
stabilito nel ciel nodo si degno.

RECITATIVO

IDOMENEO
O ciel pietoso!

IDAMANTE
Ilia . . .

ILIA
Idamante, udisti?

ARBACE
Oh gioja, oh amor, oh Numi!

ELETTRA
Oh smania! Oh furie!
Oh disperata Elettra!
Vedrò Idamante alla rivale in braccio?
Ah no, il germano Oreste
ne' cupi abissi io vuò seguir.
Or' or compagna m'avrai là nell'
inferno, a sempiterni guai, al pianto
eterno.

29. ARIA

ELETTRA
D'Oreste e d'Ajace
ho in seno i tormenti,
d'Aletto la face
già morte mi dà.
Squarciatemi il core,
ceraste serpenti,
o un ferro il dolore
in me finirà.

28. THE VOICE

Love has triumphed . . .
Heaven pardons Idomeneo for his great
offence, but not the king. It is not meet
that he should fail his promises.
He shall cease to reign; Idamante
shall be king, and Ilia his bride . . .
Then will Neptune be appeased,
heaven contented and innocence rewarded.
This worthy marriage, arranged in heaven,
will restore peace to the kingdom of Crete.

RECITATIVE

IDOMENEO
O merciful heaven!

IDAMANTE
Ilia . . .

ILIA
Idamante, did you hear?

ARBACE
O joy! What love, ye gods!

ELECTRA
O madness! Ye furies!
Despairing Electra,
Must I see Idamante in my rival's arms?
Ah no, let me follow
my brother Orestes into the hollow abyss.
Now you will have me for companion in
Hades, in eternal woe, in endless
lamenting.

29. ARIA

ELECTRA
Within my breast I feel
the torments of Orestes and of Ajax;
Alecto's torch
brings me death.
Tear out my heart,
you horned serpents,
or a sword
shall end my pain.

30. FINALE

30. FINALE

RECITATIVO

IDOMENEO
Popoli! A voi l'ultima legge
impone Idomeneo qual rè.
Pace v'annunzio. Compiuto
è il sacrifizio, e sciolto il voto.
Nettuno e tutti i Numi
a questo regno amici sòn.
Resta, che al cenno loro
Idomeneo ora ubbidisca.
O quanto, o sommi Dei,
m'è grato il cenno!
Eccovi un altro rè, un altro me
stesso. A Idamante mio figlio, al caro
figlio, cedo il soglio di Creta
e tutto insieme il sovrano poter.
I suoi comandi rispettate,
eseguite ubbidienti,
come i miei seguiste e rispettaste,
onde grato io vi son!
Questa è la legge:
eccovi la real sposa!
Mirate in questa bella coppia
un don del cielo serbato a voi.
Quanto a sperar vi lice!
O Creta fortunata! O me felice!

31. ARIA

IDOMENEO
Torna la pace al core,
torna lo spento ardore;
florisce in me l'età.
Tal la stagion di Flora
l'albero annoso infiora,
nuovo vigor gli dà.

32. CORO

Scenda Amor, scenda Imeneo,
e Giunone ai regi sposi;
d'alma pace omai li posi,
la Dea pronuba nel sen.

30. FINAL SCENE

RECITATIVE

IDOMENEO
My people! Idomeneo gives you
his last command as king.
I announce peace. The sacrifice
is completed, my vow redeemed.
Neptune and all the gods
smile upon this kingdom.
One thing remains, that Idomeneo
now obey their demand.
O mighty gods, how I welcome your
command! Here is another king for you,
my other self.
To Idamante my son, my dear son,
I relinquish the throne of Crete
together with all sovereign power.
Respect his commands.
and follow them obediently,
as you have followed and respected mine,
for which I am grateful to you!
Thus I now order:
and here is the royal bride!
Behold in this handsome pair
a gift bestowed on you by heaven.
You have so much to hope for!
O fortunate Crete! What happiness to me!

31. ARIA

IDOMENEO
Peace returns to my heart
and extinguished ardour is rekindled;
youth is reborn in me.
Thus does Flora's season
make the old tree bloom again
and give it fresh vigour.

32. CHORUS

Descend, Love and Hymen,
descend, Juno, to the royal pair;
benign goddess, now instil
the peace of your spirit in their breasts.

English translation copyright by Lionel Salter

Discography

(All English disc numbers are given in roman type; *all USA numbers in italic type*)

DON GIOVANNI

(a) Complete sets

	Set A	Set B	Set C
DON GIOVANNI	Bacquier	Ghiaurov	Fischer-Dieskau
DONNA ANNA	Sutherland	Watson	Nilsson
DON OTTAVIO	Krenn	Gedda	Schreier
DONNA ELVIRA	Lorengar	Ludwig	Arroyo
LEPORELLO	Gramm	Berry	Flagello
COMMENDATORE	Grant	Crass	Talvela
MASETTO	Monreale	Montarsolo	Mariotti
ZERLINA	M. Horne	Freni	Grist
Ensemble	English Chamber	Philharmonia	Prague
Conductor	Bonynge	Klemperer	Böhm
Disc Nos.	Dec.SET412/5	*H/SAN172/5*	DGG139260/3
	London 1434	*(Angel S3700)*	*DGG139260/3*
			(DGG2711006)

	Set D	Set E	Set F
DON GIOVANNI	Siepi	Taddei	Siepi
DONNA ANNA	Danco	Curtis Verna	Nilsson
DON OTTAVIO	Dermota	Valletti	Valletti
DONNA ELVIRA	della Casa	Cavazzi	L. Price
LEPORELLO	Corena	Tajo	Corena
COMMENDATORE	Böhme	Susca	
MASETTO	Berry	Zerbini	
ZERLINA	Güden	Ribetti	Ratti
Ensemble	Vienna	R.A. Ital.	Vienna
Conductor	Krips	Rudolf	Leinsdorf
Disc Nos.	Dec.SXL2117/20	Cet LPC1253	RE25028/31
	London 1401	*Ev-Cet 7403*	*RCA LD6410/LSC6410*

	Set G	Set H	Set I
DON GIOVANNI	Brownlee	Fischer-Dieskau	London
DONNA ANNA	Souez	Jurinac	Zadek
DON OTTAVIO	Pataky	Häfliger	Simoneau
DONNA ELVIRA	Helletsgruber	Stader	Jurinac
LEPORELLO	Baccaloni	Sardi	Weber
COMMENDATORE	Franklin	Kohn	
MASETTO	Roy Henderson	Kreppel	Berry
ZERLINA	Mildmay	Seefried	Sciutti
Ensemble	Glyndebourne	Berlin	Vienna
Conductor	Fritz Busch	Fricsay	Moralt
Disc Nos.	E/80598/600	DGG138050/52	Philips (various)
	Turn 4117/9	*Amer Decca*	*Ph/PHC3-009*

	Set J	Set K	Set L
DON GIOVANNI	Campo	Wächter	Stabile
DONNA ANNA	Danco	Sutherland	Grob-Prandl
DON OTTAVIO	Gedda	Alva	Handt
DONNA ELVIRA	Stich-Randall	Schwarzkopf	Konetzni
LEPORELLO	Cortis	Taddei	Pernersdorfer
COMMENDATORE		Frick	
MASETTO	Vessieres	Cappuccilli	Poell
ZERLINA	Moffo	Sciutti	Heusser
Ensemble	Aix en Provence	Philharmonia	Vienna
Conductor	Rosbaud	Giulini	Swarorsky
Disc Nos.	Vox OPBX162	SAX2369/72	Nixa HLP
	Vox OPBX162	*Angel S3605*	*Erato LDE3002/4*

The more recent editions may also be found in tape or cassette format. Sets A.B. C.D.F.H. & K. are stereo editions, but Set F, out of print in England, was only released there as a mono set. Set E is available in the U.S.A. as a 'stereophonic transcription'. Set G is a transfer from 78rpm records, but despite 'period' sound is still much in demand for style and authority. Sets E.F.H.I.J.L. may be regarded as obsolete.

(b) Highlight editions

Single LPs have been produced from most of the above sets, but are only variously in production in diverse European and American countries.

(c) Arias included in Artists' recitals

Ho capito Hermann Prey SAX5293
Madamina Geraint Evans SXL6262 *(OS-25994)*, Theo Adam *(S-43118)*
Or Sai chi l'onore Leontyne Price DB6742, Rita Streich (Ger.) 125020,
    Maria Callas WRCT690
Dalla sua pace Fritz Wunderlich HQS1168 *(SBB-3751)*
Finch' han dal vino Hermann Prey SAX5293 *(S-36481)* Gerard Souzay SAL3574
Deh, vieni alla finestra Hermann Prey SAX5293 *(S-36481)*,
    Gerard Souzay SAL3574, Theo Adam *(S-43118)*, Tom Krause *(OS-26042)*
Il mio tesoro Fritz Wunderlich HQS1168 *(SBB-3751)* Jussi Björling RB16011
Mi tradi Maria Callas WRCT690
Non mi dir Maria Callas WRCT690
Metà di vuoi Hermann Prey SAX5293 *(S-36481)*

(d) Selections by Historical Singers

Many hundreds of 78 rpm recordings of arias and duets from *Don Giovanni* were made between 1900 and 1950. A great number were ephemeral, but some captured the interpretations of great performers of their day, and a selection of the best of them is listed below. A remarkably high proportion have been transferred onto LP recitals, and LP numbers are shown where they are currently listed. Even where no LP number is shown, interested collectors should consult the specialist record shops, as new 'Historic' re-issues appear every month in most European countries and in the U.S.A.

Notte e giorno Mayr LV1. (Ger) *(SC822)*
Madamina Mayr LV1. (Ger). Kunz, Tajo, Pasero QALP10409, Baccaloni,
    Pinza *(LM1751)* Chaliapin H1002. Panzéra (Fr). Vanni-Marcoux, Journet,
    Fugere (Fr), Schöffler, Christoff, Rossi-Lemeni, Székely (Hun), Kipnis LV5 (Ger).
La ci darem dal Monte & Beuf QALP10415, Rethberg & Pinza, *(LM2628)* Perras
    & Hüsch (Ger), Bettendorf & Hüsch (Ger), Raisa & Rimini, Battistini & Corsi
    (SC831) Berger & Schlusnus (Ger), Belmas & Pernet (Fr).
Or sai chi l'onore Bampton, Traubel, Frida Leider LV30, *(Eterna 745, SC835)*,
    Welitsch 61088. Lilli Lehmann LPX8005 *(Eterna 743, SC826)*
Dalla sua pace Bonci, de Lucia, Tauber, Gigli HQM1075, Schitz MOAK2,
    Dermota, Schipa, Nash, Anders, Patzak LV31, Pataky, Ludwig E83385,
    Roswange SC840, Tauber *(SC837)*
Finch' han dal vino d'Andrade, Battistini, *(SC831)* Pinza VIC1470, Hüsch, Stabile,
    Panzéra, Schlusnus (Ger), Pernet, de Luca, Rossi-Lemeni, Tibbett, Sved,
    Scotti, Sammarco.
Batti, batti Seefried, Pagliughi, Sayão, Bori, Elisabeth Schumann COLH154,
    Cebotari, Rethberg, Kurz, Streich, Schwarzkopf, Farrar, Patti ORL212,
    Tetrazzini ORL210. Ponselle A125
Deh, vieni alla finestra Maurel ORE202, Battistini *(SC831)*, Siepi, Pinza
    VIC1470, Schöffler, Silveri, Gobbi, Hüsch (Ger), Baklanoff, Vanni-Marcoux,
    Domgraf-Fassbänder, Stabile, Taddei, Schlusnus (Ger), Pernet (Fr),
    Renaud *(Eterna 757* Fr. & It.). Rossi-Lemeni, Sved (Hun), Duhan LV10 (Ger),
    Schorr *(SC842)*
Vedrai carino Sayão, Güden, Bori, Elisabeth Schumann COLH154, Favero,
    Cebotari, Rita Streich, Schwarzkopf
Ah pieta, signori miei Baccaloni

Il mio tesoro de Lucia, McCormack *(LM2631)*, Schitz, Moak, Tauber, Gigli
   HQM1075, de Muro Lomanto, Crooks, Schipa, Nash, Pataky, Anders (Ger),
   Patzak (Ger), Roswänge (Ger), Villabella (Fr), Devries (Fr), Dermota,
Valletti, Simoneau, Jadlowker CO312 *(SC839)*
Mi tradi Schwarzkopf, Joan Hammond, Huni-Mihacsek (Ger).
Non mir dir Cebotari, Hampton, Norena (Fr), Huni-Mihacsek (Ger), Welitsch,
   Lilli Lehmann LPX8005 *(Eterna 702)* Schwarzkopf, Kemp CL506 (Ger).

IDOMENEO

(a) Complete sets

IDOMENEO	Shirley	R. Lewis
IDAMANTE	R. Davies	Simoneau
ILIA	Rinaldi	Jurinac
ELECTRA	Tinsley	Udovick
ARBACE	Tear	Milligan
HIGH PRIEST	Pilley	McAlpine
NEPTUNE	Dean	Alan
Ensemble	BBC London	Glyndebourne
Conductor	Colin Davis	Pritchard
Disc Nos.	SAL3747/9	SOC2013
	Ph/3747/9	*Sera S6070*

IDOMENEO	Taubmann	Klarwein
IDAMANTE	Menzel	Riedner
ILIA	G. Hopf	Cunitz
ELECTRA	Grob-Prandl	Schech
ARBACE	Handt	Lins
HIGH PRIEST	Majkut	Messerschmidt
NEPTUNE	Heiller	Eibel
Ensemble	Vienna	Bavarian Radio
Conductor	Zallinger	Altmann
	HLP2020	
	HSLP2020	*Mer MGL5.*
		(abridged on 2 LPs)

(b) Highlight editions

Glyndebourne/Pritchard (see above) SOH204, *HSLP2042*
Glyndebourne/Busch. R. Lewis. Jurinac, McNeil. A Young. *LHMV1021*,
   FALP389 (France). In GB issued on 78rpm only DB21525/9.

(c) Arias included in Artists' recitals

Famous singers who recorded arias, some of whom may be found on LP recitals,
   include Spoorenberg, Leontyne Price, Hilde Güden, Zadak, Stich-Randall,
   Jadlowker, Schwarzkopf, Tourel, Ginster, Erna Berger, Piltti, Vera Schwarz.
Note: the abridged recording conducted by Altmann is from the edition of the
score edited by Wolf-Ferrari.